# Knott's Berry Farm Cookbook

By Florine Sikking and Judith Zeidler

Armstrong Publishing

*First Printing:* May 1976
*Fifth Printing:* 1981

Copyright © 1976 by Knott's Berry Farm
Library of Congress Catalog Card Number: 76-5752
Printed in the United States of America
All rights reserved
ISBN: 0-915936-03-8

*Recipes by:* Brentwood Culinary Consultants

*Book Design by:* Graphics Two

*Illustrations by:* Betty Billups

*Published by:* Armstrong Publishing Company
     5514 Wilshire Boulevard
     Los Angeles, California 90036

# Contents

The Knott's Story  5

A Cookbook for Pioneers  9

Knott's Specialty Foods  10

Mrs. Knott's Recipes  13

Ghost Town  25

Fiesta Village  55

Roaring 20's  77

Independence Hall  109

Food & Wine: A Celebration of Life  120

Metric System Weights & Measures  122

Index  123

"It All Started Out So Simply . . ."

# The Knott's Story

*Cordelia and Walter*

It all started out so simply and inauspiciously. On a dusty road right next to Walter and Cordelia Knott's struggling produce fields, a little berry stand was put up one day in 1920 in an effort to augment the farming family's meager income. Times were tough, and the first few years were unkind ones. But unknown to them then, the Knotts inherently held the secret keys to business success — ingenuity, perseverance, togetherness, and dedication to hard work. It worked. The berries Walter grew with so much labor and love became the talk of his neighborhood, then of his town of Buena Park, then of his county of Orange, and then throughout the whole of Southern California. Knott's great berries were a "must stop and buy some" for both old friends and for travelers and tourists who had heard the good news by word of mouth. The berries flourished, the number of purchasing passersby increased, the stand prospered, and Knott family efforts grew ever more fruitful and rewarding.

The big Depression hit then, in 1928, but the Knotts responded positively by using the last of their savings to build the Farm's first permanent business building — a combined berry market, a small nursery to sell berry plants, and a five-table Tea Room where Cordelia served sandwiches, hot biscuits with berry

Circa 1935, son Russell learns from "the expert."

*As the number of diners grew, so did the Farm and the Restaurant.*

jam, and fresh berry pie. The family's home was attached to the back of the Tea Room and cooking for the small eating place was done in the family kitchen. Walter and Cordelia lived in that same house in the center of the Farm's activities until Cordelia's death in April 1974.

Even in those difficult years, the Knotts and their expanding activities continued to succeed. In fact, Walter first cultivated and then introduced the revolutionary Boysenberry in 1935. This spectacular new fruit — a cross of a loganberry, a blackberry and a red raspberry — was named after Walter's Anaheim neighbor Rudolph Boysen, the originator. About that time, Cordelia became contrary in her running of the Tea Room — luckily for all. After repeated warnings to Walter that "we're not going into the restaurant business," she reversed herself completely and on a whim decided to add to the menu and "try some chicken dinners," her specialty. So on one fateful summer day in 1934, served on her wedding china, she presented her first commercial chicken dinners to eight very appreciative guests. The Knott daughters, Virginia, Toni and Marion, helped in the dining room and Mrs. Knott supervised all cooking. Neighborhood women staffed the kitchen and local girls served as waitresses.

Continued growth followed this instant acceptance. In 1937 a 300-seat restaurant was built to meet the surging demand, and by 1940 some 400,000 dinners were served in that single year — as much as 4,000 on a single Sunday.

*Early autos brought hungry visitors from all over the country.*

1940 was another milestone year — Ghost Town was begun by Walter as a tribute to his pioneering grandparents and his love of the Old West, and also to entertain the long lines of impatient customers awaiting their homemade chicken dinners. His initial acquisition — the authentic Gold Trails Hotel, originally built in 1868 near Prescott, Arizona — became but the first of some 100 attractions and rides at Knott's Berry Farm today. Further additions to the Farm continued during the 1960's with the opening of the Calico Mine Ride, the Timber Mountain Log Ride and Knott's second "Old Time Adventures" themed area: Fiesta Village, which offers all the festivity and colorful excitement of early California. As Knott's "Old Time Adventures" and the Chicken Dinner Restaurant grew, shops, stores and other eating facilities were added. Today the original 20-acre Berry Farm is 150 acres and employs more than 3,000 persons during the summer.

Knott's has continued to expand and in 1975 opened the "Roaring 20's" amusement area, a five-acre addition designed to recreate the fun and excitement of a 1920's California amusement park.

Ten Knott family members, spanning three generations, own and operate this world-famous entertainment complex which attracts six million visitors annually. All ten adhere to Walter's deeply-held concepts of hard work, honesty and thrift, along with the belief that the essential goodness of man will eventually triumph.

# A Cookbook for Pioneers

Pioneers are special people. You'll find them busy opening strange doors, discovering new places and things, or busting through old barriers. A good example is Walter and Cordelia Knott. Even in these 20th Century days, they were true pioneers — in farming and berry development, in cooking and the art of preserving, in showmanship and entertainment. They were exceptional. But all of us are pioneers at heart, in one way or another. We all do things differently — only some more daringly and with a little more dash than others. It's all in how you look at it. In any event, pioneers need good foods well prepared to properly fuel our energetic efforts. This means good, fresh, nutritional, nourishing foods which are balanced in content value but varied in flavors and styles. Our "KNOTT'S BERRY FARM COOKBOOK" is carefully constructed for all the pioneers in your family — young, medium or old. Like good ingredients, our innovative recipes are fresh and wholesome. They reflect pioneering instincts in being daring and different. They're minor Old Time Adventures in eating, modernized for today's new tastes. So try them and discover for yourself a new world of difference in dining.

# Knott's Speciality Foods

Knott's extensive line of specialty foods and quality preserving products is the end result of its jams, jellies, syrups, dressings, pickles, sauces and relishes starting out as freshly prepared garnishes in the Chicken Dinner Restaurant and Steak House. They were finally offered for sale to meet steady public demand, and over the years millions of visitors have taken or mailed home some of these delicious table delicacies.

Popularity of Knott's products and gift packages has grown so fast and so great that it now takes seven food specialty shops (three markets, three candy shops and a bakery) on the Farm to fully satisfy this expanding demand.

Outside interest was first tested at several gourmet shops, and today the Knott's food line is marketed successfully throughout the U.S., Canada and Japan. This manufactured food line has expanded to include 20 flavors of preserves, seven jellies, seven dressings, five fruit syrups and a specialty sauce and relish. Other items carrying the Knott's label but made elsewhere under strict quality control specifications are nut butters, flours, olives, honeys and spiced fruits.

Distinct difference and evident quality are the two good reasons why Knott's line of preserves are capturing an ever-increasing share of market. The secret is the use of the finest fruit obtainable cooked in small, carefully-watched batches in open kettles. This as opposed to the mass-produced method of vacuum-cooking tons of fruit at one time to save time and money at the expense of flavor and quality.

A large share of Knott's food business, especially the sale of its sought-after gift packs, is done by mail order. Each year hundreds of thousands of items are mailed throughout the U.S. and overseas to most of the Free World, all guaranteed to arrive safely, in the proper condition and on time. Knott's catalogs are also mailed out annually to customers by request.

Should you be unable to find at your local shopping center any of the specific Knott's products included in these recipes, please write to our: Preserving Office, Knott's Berry Farm, 8039 Beach Blvd., Buena Park, Cal. 90620.

Mrs. Knott's Fried Chicken Dinner

Mrs. Knott's Boysenberry Pie

# The Magic Chicken Dinner Formula

That chicken dinner first offered by Cordelia Knott and her daughters in the harsh Depression days of 1934 turned out to be a magic and winning formula. Cherry rhubarb served in sauce dishes was brought out first as the hors d'oeuvre. Then came green salad with French dressing. The main course consisted of fried chicken, mashed potatoes with milk gravy, boiled cabbage with bits of ham, and hot biscuits served with jam. Dessert was cut from Cordelia's deep, 10-inch berry pies — and most usually her famous Boysenberry pie.

Today that dinner is still the all-time favorite at the Farm. The price has increased only in proportion to living costs through the years. And the same words of appreciation and accompanying smiles of satisfaction that were given by the first eight customers in 1934 are repeated today by thousands.

Cordelia modestly disclaimed any secret formula for her chicken dinners that lured so many customers from near and far. "It's just homemade, just like you'd make it yourself," she'd repeat to inquiries.

But for those of us who might need a helping-hand guide to duplicate her accomplishment, here are the exact recipes we have used through the years, offered publicly for the very first time.

# Navy Bean Soup

- 1 ham bone
- ½ pound ham, diced
- 2 quarts chicken stock
- 1 1-pound package white navy beans
- ½ teaspoon garlic powder or 2 cloves garlic, minced
- 2 onions, diced
- ½ cup celery, diced
- ½ cup carrots, diced
- 4 tomatoes, diced
- 2 tablespoons tomato paste
- 1 bay leaf
- 1 teaspoon thyme
- salt and white pepper to taste

In a large Dutch oven or soup pot, place ham bone and diced ham and chicken stock. Simmer for ½ an hour. Rinse beans and add to Dutch oven with all the remaining ingredients. Bring to a boil, lower heat and simmer about 1½ to 2 hours or until beans are very soft. Add additional stock if soup becomes too thick or simmer longer if soup is too liquid, or add roux (2 tablespoons flour to 1 tablespoon oil) if you desire. Serve garnished with parsley.

**Serves 6-8**

# Cherry Rhubarb Sauce

- 1 pound cherry rhubarb, cut in 1-inch slices
- 1½ cups sugar
- 2¼ cups water

Place rhubarb in a large saucepan, pour sugar over and let stand 1 hour. Add water to mixture in saucepan and bring to a boil slowly, uncovered, and cook 1 to 5 minutes until rhubarb is soft.

Cool, cover and refrigerate several hours before serving.

**Serves 6**

# Mrs. Knott's Salad

- ½ head iceberg lettuce
- 3 radishes, diced
- 1 carrot, peeled and diced
  Knott's French Dressing

Wash lettuce and dry thoroughly. Lettuce becomes brown when it is not dried completely. Wrap lettuce in paper towels which will absorb any remaining moisture on lettuce. Put in crisper section of refrigerator. When ready to serve salad, tear lettuce into bite-size pieces and combine with radishes and carrot. Pour in desired amount of dressing and toss well to evenly coat the lettuce. Serve immediately.

**Serves 4**

# Cabbage With Ham

- 3 cups water
- 1 head cabbage, shredded
  salt to taste
- 1 cup ham, cooked and chopped

In a 6-quart saucepan, pour in water then add cabbage and salt and bring to a boil. Reduce heat and simmer covered for 4 minutes or until just tender. Drain almost all of the liquid, then add ham and toss well. Serve in a side dish to accompany fried chicken.

**Serves 6-8**

# Chicken Salad

- 4 cups chicken, cooked and diced
- ½ cup celery, chopped
- 2 eggs, hard cooked
- dash white pepper
- ¼ cup sweet pickle relish
- 1 cup mayonnaise
- salt to taste

In a large bowl, combine chicken, celery, eggs and pepper and toss well. Add pickle relish and blend in mayonnaise. Add salt to taste. Should you wish a more moist salad, add additional mayonnaise. Chill well.

**Serves 6**

# Buttermilk Biscuits

*Millions of biscuits have been made with Cordelia's own rolling pin.*

1½ cups all-purpose flour
 2 tablespoons baking powder (double acting)*
    pinch of salt
 1 tablespoon solid shortening
    pinch baking soda (or ⅛ teaspoon)
 1 cup buttermilk

    cottonseed or vegetable oil

In an electric mixer, combine flour, baking powder, salt, and shortening and mix until consistency of coarse meal. Combine baking soda and buttermilk in a seperate bowl and beat with a spoon until foamy and thickened. Add buttermilk mixture to flour and beat until well blended. Do not overbeat. Mixture will be sticky.

Turn out onto a well-floured board, sprinkle top of dough with flour, and pat until one-inch thick. Pour enough oil into jelly roll-type pan (approximately 11" x 7") to measure ¼ inch (or about ¼ cup oil). In a second pan pour an equal amount of oil. Cut biscuits with cookie cutter** or drinking glass and roll each biscuit in the first pan of oil, then place in second pan. (Oil will cling to dough, which is desirable.) Continue cutting and rolling in oil until second pan is filled. Biscuits should be touching each other. Pat top of biscuits with oil from first pan. Bake in preheated 500° oven for 10-12 minutes or until golden brown.

*Make sure that the baking powder is fresh. Baking powder loses its effectiveness when stored for a long period of time.

**Makes approximately 18 2" biscuits or 20 1¾" biscuits or 30 1½" biscuits

# Mashed Potatoes & Chicken Gravy

- 4 medium potatoes, peeled and quartered
  water to cover
- ¼ cup butter or margarine
- 4-6 tablespoons milk
- ½ teaspoon salt

Boil potatoes in water in a covered saucepan until tender when pierced with a fork. Drain potatoes and mash potatoes with masher or with an electric mixer. Add butter and blend until butter has melted. Add milk and salt and continue whipping until potatoes are light and fluffy.

**Serves 6**

- chicken drippings
- ¼ cup flour
- 1 cup milk
- salt to taste
- ¼ cup chicken, cooked and ground

Scrape pan with wooden spoon to release all crusty drippings left from frying chicken. Add flour to drippings and blend over low heat until ingredients are combined and flour is lightly browned. Add milk and salt and cook over low heat for 5 minutes, stirring regularly. Add chicken and mix well. Serve immediately spooned over mashed potatoes.

**Yields 1½ cups**

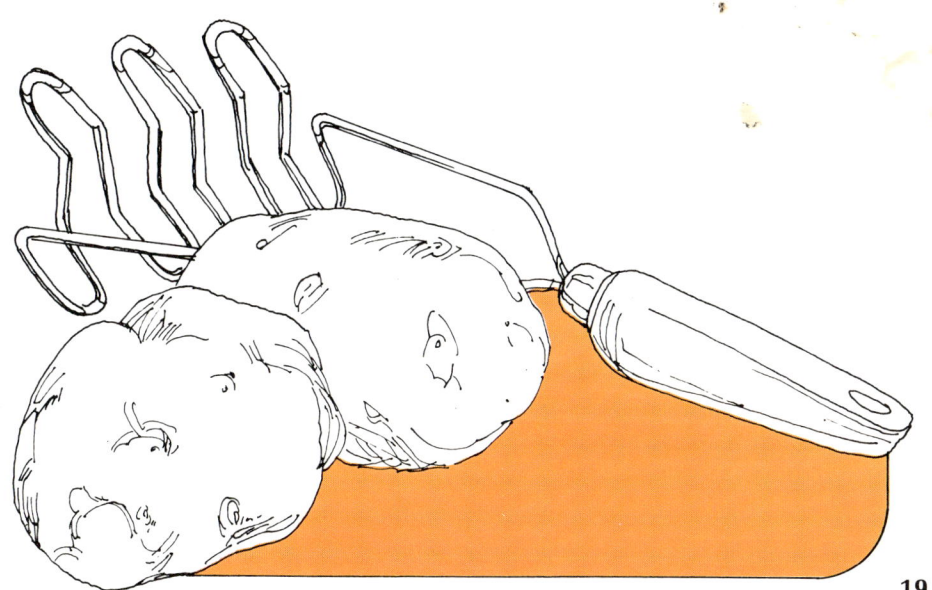

# Chicken Livers

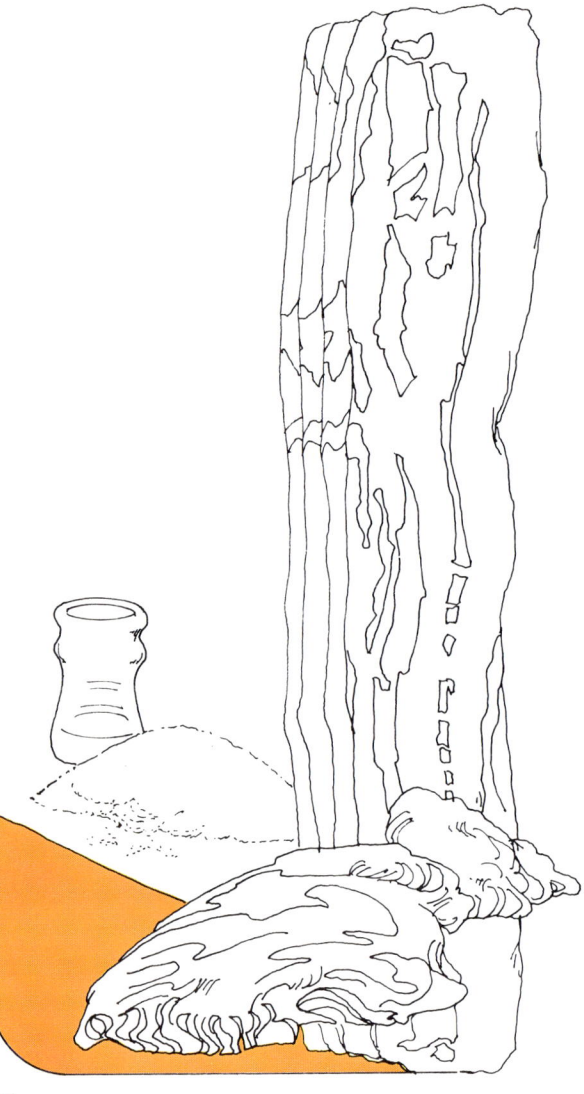

- 1 cup flour
- dash of white pepper
- ½ teaspoon salt
- ¼ teaspoon garlic powder
- 2 pounds chicken livers
- 2 tablespoons bacon, cooked and crumbled, or bacon bits

**vegetable oil for deep frying**

In a brown bag, combine all ingredients except livers and bacon. Shake in closed bag to mix ingredients. Drop in a few livers at a time and shake bag, coating livers. Remove and continue coating remaining livers.

Heat oil to 350° and drop in livers, a few at a time, and cook 5 minutes or until livers are no longer pink in center. Drain on paper towels. Toss in crumbled bacon and serve immediately.

**Serves 6**

# Fried Chicken

- 2  3-pound frying chickens, cut in eighths
- 2  cups unbleached flour
- 1  quart oil (or enough to cover chicken)

Cover chicken with salted water and soak for 45 minutes. Drain chicken and pat dry. Coat each piece of chicken with flour and shake off any excess flour. Bring oil to a boil in an 8½-quart saucepan and drop in chicken pieces. (Do not overcrowd chicken in the pot.) Cover and fry for 45 minutes. Remove chicken with slotted spoon and drain on paper towels. Fifteen minutes before serving, heat ¼ cup oil in a large skillet and re-fry chicken for 3 minutes.

**Serves 6**

*Everyone enjoys Mrs. Knott's fried chicken.*

# Steak House Beef Stew

*Our well-known Steak House on the Farm where visitors enjoy this stew.*

¼ cup oil
2 medium onions, sliced
3 cloves garlic, minced
4 pounds stew meat
1 28-ounce can tomatoes with liquid
1 cup dry red wine
2 tablespoons Worcestershire sauce
1 bay leaf
1 teaspoon basil, crushed
1 tablespoon parsley, chopped
salt and pepper to taste

2 potatoes, diced
3 pounds carrots, diced
3 stalks celery, diced
1 16-ounce can corn, drained
1 15-ounce can lima beans, drained

In a large Dutch oven, heat oil and saute onions and garlic until soft. Add meat and brown on all sides. Add tomatoes, wine, Worcestershire sauce, bay leaf, basil, parsley, salt and pepper. Simmer partially covered for 1 hour.

In the meantime, combine potatoes, carrots and celery in a saucepan with 1 cup water and cook until a little tender but still firm. After meat has simmered for an hour, add these vegetables and the remaining ingredients. Continue cooking until meat is tender.

**Serves 8-10**

# Mrs. Knott's Boysenberry Pie

7½ ounces water
6½ ounces sugar
   dash of salt
1 tablespoon corn syrup
1 teaspoon lemon juice

3 tablespoons cornstarch
2 ounces water
1 16-ounce bag frozen boysenberries (do not thaw)

2 **crust pie shell** (see recipe for "Flapper's Fruity Tarts" in Roaring 20's section)

In a saucepan, combine water, sugar, salt, corn syrup and lemon juice and bring to a boil.

Combine cornstarch and water and blend thoroughly. Add to saucepan and mix well. Heat thoroughly. Add frozen boysenberries. Pour into unbaked 9-inch pie crust. Cover with second top crust and seal well around the edges. Make several slashes in the top to release steam. Bake in a preheated 400° oven for 40 minutes or until top is golden brown. Cool on a rack.

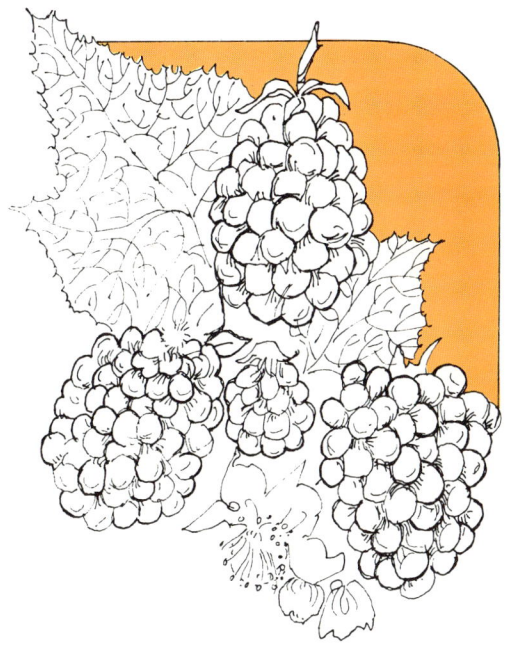

Silver Dollar Cucumber Salad, Russian River Eggs garnished with Calico Carrots, Campsite Corn Relish

Prospector's Pork Tenderloin, Rancher's Marinated Chicken Livers, Branding Iron Meatballs

Knott's first Old Time Adventure, since 1940 — is a life-like reflection of the rootin'-tootin', gun-totin', rip-roarin' 49er days of the Wild West. A bustling Gold Rush town is wholly recreated with an authentic collection of old ghost town buildings, shops and folklore. Here you're cordially invited to swagger down rustic wooden boardwalks, climb aboard a stagecoach, take a wild log ride if you dare, quench your thirst with sarsaparilla in the brass-railed Calico Saloon, hiss the villain at a melodrama in the Bird Cage Theatre, ride a rickety train car through the Calico Gold Mine, tiptoe up Boot Hill and through the Haunted Shack, pan for real gold, catch the Covered Wagon Show, get held up aboard the Denver and Rio Grande steam-powered narrow-gauge Calico Railroad, zero in on a bull's-eye at the Shootin' Gallery, or simply set a spell on the porch of the 100-year-old-plus Gold Trails Hotel. In this section of our cookbook, we feature the more basic and country-style recipes — with emphasis on nutritional meals, natural foods and home-baked breads.

# Ghost Town Meal-In-A-Soup

Old Red Cliff, No. 41, pulls into Ghost Town with the daring Log Ride nearby.

Get real hungry to fully enjoy this meat and soup in a pot. Veal is our choice because of its milder meat flavor, but beef can easily be substituted.

- 3 pounds veal (top round)
- 3 marrow bones (cut in thirds)
- 3 quarts water
- 1 tablespoon salt
- 1 onion, sliced
- 6 carrots, sliced
- 2 medium potatoes, peeled and chunked
- 1 turnip, chopped
- 2 parsnips, chopped
- 4 leeks, sliced
- 1 celery stalk, sliced
- 1 sprig parsley, chopped
- 1 sprig of thyme (½ teaspoon dried)
- 12 peppercorns
- salt and pepper to taste

Place veal and marrow bones in a large saucepan or Dutch oven, add water and salt and bring to a boil. Skim off foam that forms on top. Add vegetables. Add parsley, thyme and peppercorns tied in a cheesecloth sack. Simmer covered on low heat for 3 hours. Uncover and simmer an additional hour or enough to reduce soup to enrich flavor. Remove cheesecloth sack. Add salt and pepper to taste and serve hot with a piece of veal, marrow and an assortment of vegetables in each bowl. Serve with thick slices of Farmer's Whole Wheat Bread — recipe found in this section.

Serves 8

# Main Street Cauliflower Soup

*Smooth and creamy, this rich soup goes well with any main dish. The optional sherry or Madeira truly enlivens hidden flavors.*

- 1 head cauliflower, about 1½ pounds
- 4 cups chicken stock

- 4 tablespoons butter
- 4 tablespoons flour
- ½ cup milk
- 2 egg yolks
- ½ cup sour cream
- 3 tablespoons butter, unsalted, melted
- ¼ cup Madeira or sherry (optional)
- salt and pepper to taste

Break cauliflower into flowerets, wash and simmer in 4 cups chicken stock for 10 minutes. Reserve 6 flowerets for garnish. Remove cauliflower with a slotted spoon and set chicken stock aside.

In a saucepan, melt butter then add flour, stirring with a wire whisk over low flame for 3 to 4 minutes. Add chicken stock and continue stirring with wire whisk and add cauliflower to saucepan. Puree cauliflower mixture in a blender and return to saucepan. Add milk and simmer, watching carefully as it must not boil.

In a small bowl, mix together egg yolks, sour cream and melted butter. Spoon some of hot soup mixture into egg yolk mixture and add this to soup, mixing constantly with wire whisk. Simmer 5 to 10 minutes. Add additional salt and pepper to taste. Madeira or sherry can be added at this point. Garnish with reserved flowerets.

Serves 6

# Silver Dollar Cucumber Salad

Main Street, as it was 100 years ago.

*Instead of the standard sour cream with cucumbers, try this refreshingly different combination of yogurt and mint jelly. Garnish each serving with a dollop of the mint jelly.*

- 1 medium clove garlic, crushed
- 1 8-ounce carton plain yogurt
- 1½ teaspoon Knott's Mint Flavored Apple Jelly
- 2 medium cucumbers, peeled and sliced thin
- ½ teaspoon salt
- 4-6 lettuce leaves

Blend garlic and yogurt together. Add 1 teaspoon mint jelly and blend thoroughly. (If jelly does not blend smoothly, press mixture through a strainer.) Stir in cucumber slices and season with salt. Serve on a bed of lettuce. Garnish with ½ teaspoon mint jelly.

**Serves 4-6**

# Campsite Corn Relish

*For barbecues or picnics, this simple-to-make relish makes a good change of pace with its sweet-and-sour natural goodness.*

½ head cabbage, shredded
1 red bell pepper, chopped
½ green bell pepper, chopped
½ cup onion, chopped
½ clove garlic
5 stalks celery, chopped
4 cups corn (canned or fresh)
¼ cup Knott's Clover Honey
1 tablespoon salt
1 tablespoon dry mustard
1 teaspoon turmeric
½ cup white vinegar (or lemon)
½ cup water

*A prospector at campsite.*

Combine cabbage, red pepper, green pepper, onion, garlic and celery in a saucepan. Add one cup water to cover and cook 5 minutes. Drain and add corn in saucepan. In a small bowl, mix together honey, salt, dry mustard and turmeric and stir in vinegar and water. Pour over vegetables and bring to a boil. Simmer for 10 minutes, stirring occasionally. Refrigerate and serve as a relish with meats.

**Yields 6 cups**

# Russian River Eggs

*The Log Ride shoots the rushing waters.*

Here's a savory solution for those leftover vegetables. Adding other favorite vegetables only enhances this practical use of hard-boiled eggs.

4-6 eggs, hard cooked (one per person)
  2 carrots, chopped small
  5 ounces frozen peas (or half a 10-ounce package)
  2 stalks celery, chopped small

⅔ cup Knott's All-Purpose Dressing
  1 heaping tablespoon French-style mustard
  1 teaspoon capers, chopped
  2 tablespoons red pimientos, chopped
  2 tablespoons chives
  ½ teaspoon celery seed
  3 drops Worcestershire sauce
  1 tablespoon white wine vinegar (or lemon juice)
    salt and pepper to taste
  1 head Bibb lettuce

Chill the eggs until ready to use. Cook carrots in boiling water until just tender, or about 10 minutes. Remove with slotted spoon and set aside in a bowl. Cook peas until just tender, or about 5 minutes. Using a slotted spoon, add peas to carrots. Drop celery into same boiling water for about 2-3 minutes. Do not overcook. Drain and add to other vegetables.

In a larger bowl, combine all remaining ingredients and mix thoroughly. Add vegetables, mix and chill thoroughly. Peel eggs, slice them or cut lengthwise into eighths. Cover bottom of each salad plate with lettuce and arrange egg on lettuce. Spoon on sauce generously.

Serves 4-6

# Calico Carrots

*How about pickling carrots for a salad? Pickling was a pioneer's trick to preserve vegetables. Today we pickle carrots for the novel flavor.*

- 24 carrots
- 1½ tablespoons pickling spices
- 1 cup vinegar
- 1 cup sugar

Cook carrots in boiling water, covered, until skins can be slipped off easily.

Place pickling spices in a cheesecloth bag or tea container. Combine vinegar, pickling spice bag and sugar in a saucepan and boil for 10 minutes to make a syrup. Remove spice bag. Put carrots in a large bowl and pour hot syrup over them. Cover and refrigerate until ready to use.

**Yields 24 carrots**

The Calico Mine Ride below hanging stalactites.

# Farmer's Whole Wheat Bread

*A farmer's friend at work.*

*Because of its many natural and wholesome ingredients, farmers made this versatile type of bread that was served anytime — at breakfast, dinner, supper and even in-between.*

- 2 packages dry yeast
- 1 teaspoon Knott's Clover or Orange Honey
- 1½ cups lukewarm water
- ¾ cup milk, warm
- ¼ cup molasses
- ¼ cup Knott's Clover or Orange Honey
- 2 tablespoons vegetable oil
- 1 tablespoon salt
- 4 cups whole-wheat flour
- 2 cups all-purpose white flour
- ½ cup pistachio nuts, chopped (optional)

Combine yeast, 1 teaspoon honey and ½ cup water in a bowl and let stand. In a large mixing bowl, combine the milk, remaining water, molasses, honey, oil and salt. Add yeast mixture and blend. Add flour, a cup at a time, blending thoroughly after each addition to a soft dough. Turn out onto a floured board and knead until smooth and elastic, about 10 minutes. Place dough in a large, greased bowl and grease top of dough. Cover with kitchen towel and let rise in a warm place until it doubles in bulk or about 1½ to 2 hours.

Punch dough down and knead in nuts. Divide dough into 2 loaves and place in well-greased 7½"x3¾"x2¼" loaf pans. Cover and let rise until double in bulk. Brush top with oil. Bake in a preheated 425° oven for 10 minutes then reduce heat to 350° and bake for 25 to 30 minutes or until done. (Tap on top and listen for a hollow sound — then bread is done.) Remove from pan, loosening sides with a spatula. Cool on a rack.

**Yields 2 loaves**

# Grist Mill Whole Wheat Muffins

*A Knott's Berry Farm original, these easy-to-make muffins go great with soups, salads or main dishes. Reheat leftovers for a next-day breakfast treat.*

- 2 cups whole wheat flour
- ½ cup sugar
- 3½ teaspoons baking powder
- ½ teaspoon salt
- 1½ cups milk
- 1 egg
- 3 tablespoons melted butter

In a large mixing bowl, combine flour, sugar, baking powder and salt. Add milk, egg and butter and blend thoroughly. Pour into 12 well greased muffin tins and bake in preheated 375° oven for 25 to 30 minutes. Serve with Knott's preserves of your choice.

**Yields 12**

*The old Grist Mill grinds away.*

# Gold Nugget Noodles

*Pan for real gold nuggets right at Ghost Town.*

*This unusual side dish, to be served with the main course, is sweetened subtly with both marmalade and raisins. Your hard-to-please kids will love it, and it could become a weekly favorite.*

½ **pound medium wide noodles**
1 **teaspoon salt**

3 **eggs, separated**
  **pinch of salt**
1 **cup sour cream**
⅔ **cup Knott's Orange Marmalade**
½ **cup white raisins**

1½ **tablespoons margarine**

Cook noodles in 4 quarts of water to which 1 teaspoon of salt has been added. When noodles are cooked but still firm, drain thoroughly.

Beat egg whites until stiff, adding pinch of salt during mixing. Set aside. Beat egg yolks, add sour cream and blend. Stir in marmalade and raisins, then add noodles. Mix until all ingredients are blended. Fold in egg whites.

Grease bottom and sides of an 8"x8"x2" glass baking dish or a 16-cup capacity mold with the margarine. Pour in mixture and bake for 35-40 minutes in a 350° oven. (If you use a mold, let stand for 5 minutes before turning out on serving platter.)

Serves 6

# Covered Wagon Camp Beans

There's no mystery here, it's the Knott's Apricot Syrup that adds that special flavor. Pair this with either the "Butterfield Stage Spareribs" or the "Railroad Tie Riblets" — both found in this section.

- 2 pounds pinto beans
- 2 quarts water
- 2 tablespoons margarine
- 1 medium onion, chopped

- ½ pound salt pork or left-over pork

- 1 cup (8 ounces) Knott's Apricot Syrup
- 1 teaspoon dry mustard
- 2 teaspoons salt
- ⅓ cup brown sugar

Wash beans thoroughly and discard any imperfect ones. Combine beans with water and bring to a boil. Reduce heat and simmer until beans are tender. Drain beans but retain ½ cup of liquid.

Melt margarine in skillet and saute onion until tender. Combine with beans. Blanch salt pork in boiling water and make several slashes in it. Place beans in a large pot, bean pot or crockpot and bury salt pork in beans.

Combine reserved liquid and remaining ingredients in a saucepan and bring to a boil. Pour mixture over beans and cook on low heat for at least 4 hours. (Chunks of vegetables can be added before cooking begins — such as carrots and parsnips.)

Serves 8-10

# Sad Eye Joe's Squash

Sad Eye Joe on a real bad day.

*For a full-bodied vegetable, you just can't beat this sweet, economical and easy-to-make dish. And remember, don't leave out the nutmeg.*

- 2 pounds squash, banana or hubbard
- 3 tablespoons margarine
- ½ cup dark brown sugar
- ¼ cup Knott's Orange or Clover Honey
  dash of nutmeg for each square of squash
  dash of salt for each square of squash

Cut squash into 3-inch by 1-inch chunks, leaving on outer peel. Place each chunk of squash on a separate square of foil, sprinkle with salt, dot with 1 teaspoon of margarine, and sprinkle generously with sugar, honey and nutmeg. Bring sides of foil together at top and seal securely. Seal ends together. Place the foil-covered squash in a long shallow glass baking dish and bake in a preheated 375° oven for 45 minutes or until a fork goes through the squash easily. May be served in the foil or removed and topped with the juices from the foil.

**Serves 6**

# Pioneer Eggplant Roll

*Substitute eggplant for pasta and discover a weightful difference. Serve this delicious year-round vegetable and even those who generally don't eat eggplant will enjoy it.*

2 eggplants, about 1 pound each
   butter and oil
1½ cups ricotta cheese
⅓ cup romano cheese, grated
1 tablespoon basil, crushed
1 clove garlic, minced
¼ teaspoon oregano, crushed
¼ teaspoon nutmeg
   salt and pepper to taste
   Tomato Sauce (recipe follows)

Cut eggplants into lengthwise slices approximately ¼ inch thick. In a large skillet lightly saute eggplant slices in a mixture of butter and oil. Drain on paper towels.

In a large bowl, mix ricotta, romano, basil, garlic, oregano, nutmeg, salt and pepper until blended. Place a spoonful of cheese mixture on narrow end of each eggplant slice and roll up. Place seam-side down on oiled baking dish in a single layer. Spoon generously with tomato sauce, sprinkle with romano cheese and bake in a preheated 375° oven for 20 minutes or until sauce is bubbling and cheese is golden.

TOMATO SAUCE:
2 tablespoons oil
2 onions, minced
4 cloves garlic, minced
1 28-ounce can whole tomatoes, pureed
   or 8 fresh tomatoes plus 1 cup beef
   stock or red wine
1 teaspoon sugar
1 teaspoon oregano
½ teaspoon basil
½ teaspoon thyme
   salt and pepper to taste

Heat oil in a skillet, saute onions and garlic until soft. Add tomatoes, sugar, oregano, basil, thyme, salt and pepper and simmer uncovered for 15-20 minutes.

**Serves 4-6**

# Gold Mine Mushrooms

Gold miners in the Glory Hole.

*Here's a rich partner for a plain meat or fish dish. For a dash of difference, make this vegetable-custard in individual custard cups.*

- 1 cup chicken stock
- ½ cup cream
- 4 eggs
- ¾ teaspoon salt
- ½ teaspoon paprika
- ⅛ teaspoon nutmeg, grated
- 1 tablespoon parsley, chopped
- 2 tablespoons butter
- 2 cups fresh mushrooms, chopped

Put stock, cream, eggs and seasonings into a bowl and beat with a wire whisk. Melt butter and saute mushrooms for 5 minutes and drain. Add mushrooms to the egg mixture and pour into 8 small buttered molds or 1 large mold and place in a pan of hot water and bake in a preheated 350° oven for 20 to 30 minutes or until firm. (Large mold requires more time.) A knife inserted in the center should come out clean.

**Serves 8**

# Calico Can-Can Casserole
### (SWEET POTATO AND APPLE)

*Who would ever think to combine sweet potatoes and apples? In this new casserole, the tartness of the apples balance the sweetness of the potatoes. It works!*

- 4 large sweet potatoes

- 4 apples, Golden Delicious or Pippins
- 1 teaspoon salt
- 2 teaspoons marjoram
- 2 teaspoons thyme
- ½ cup Knott's Orange Blossom Honey
- 4 tablespoons butter

*Real live high-kickin' Can-Can Girls in Ghost Town.*

Place whole, unpeeled potatoes in a saucepan, cover with water and bring to a boil. Cover saucepan and cook on medium heat until potatoes are tender or about 30 minutes. When cool, remove and peel. Set aside.

Core, peel and slice apples and saute in butter until soft and slightly brown. Cut cold sweet potatoes into ¾-inch slices. Butter a baking dish and layer potatoes and apples, sprinkle with salt, marjoram and thyme. Pour honey over potato-apple mixture and dot with butter. Bake in a preheated 375° oven for 30 minutes or until apples are brown and syrup is absorbed.

**Serves 6-8**

# Sage Brush Sole

Getting ready for the desert sand and sage brush are two old miners with their burro.

Its name gives its secret away. This unusual use of sage with fish adds a new dimension to the versatile sole. The grapes make a perfect marriage here.

SOLE:
2 pounds fillet of sole
4 tablespoons butter or margarine
2 tablespoons lemon juice
  salt and pepper to taste

In a large skillet, saute sole in butter and season with lemon, salt and pepper. Cook for 5 minutes, turn fish over and continue cooking an additional 5 minutes. Serve sole on individual plates and spoon on sauce.

SAUCE:
2 tablespoons butter or margarine
1 tablespoon flour
1 teaspoon sage, crushed
1 8-ounce can grapes
¼ cup Knott's Sage Blossom Honey
4 tablespoons lemon juice
¼ teaspoon salt

Melt butter in a saucepan and add flour blending into a paste. Add sage and cook for 3 minutes. Drain grapes and reserve ¼ cup liquid. Set grapes aside. Add ¼ cup liquid to saucepan and stir until thoroughly blended. Add honey and mix well, then add lemon juice and salt and continue mixing. Add grapes and cook partially covered for 10 minutes.

**Serves 6**

# Stage Coach Stuffing

*Just glance at these uncommon dressing ingredients and you'll begin to appreciate just how special anything stuffed with it will be.*

1 pound fresh chestnuts or 2 6-ounce cans water chestnuts, chopped

1½ pounds ground beef
8 ounces pork sausage (bulk)
1 cup onions, chopped
1 cup celery, chopped
3 cups chicken broth
1 cup rice, uncooked
1 cup raisins
½ cup slivered almonds
1½ teaspoons salt
1 teaspoon ground cinnamon
¼ teaspoon pepper
2 eggs, beaten

Cut slash in fresh chestnuts with sharp knife. Place on baking sheet. Roast in 450° oven for 6 minutes. Cool, peel and chop.

In a 12-inch skillet, cook ground beef, sausage, onion and celery until meat is browned and vegetables are tender. Remove from heat. Add broth, chestnuts, rice, raisins, almonds, salt, cinnamon and pepper. Return to heat. Cover, simmer for 30 minutes. Remove from heat and add eggs to meat mixture and blend thoroughly. Stuff loosely into turkey or chickens and sew up both openings.

**Yields 9 cups stuffing**

TO PREPARE CHICKENS:
4 3½-pound chickens
4 tablespoons margarine
3 teaspoons salt
3 teaspoons onion powder
2 teaspoons cinnamon
¼ cup white wine
3 tablespoons Knott's Currant or Apple Jelly
½ cup chicken stock or water

Spread margarine on chickens, sprinkle evenly with salt, onion powder and cinnamon. Combine wine, jelly and stock and blend thoroughly. Pour liquid mixture into bottom of roasting pan or glass baking dishes and place chicken breast side down. Cook in 350° oven for one hour, basting every 20 minutes.

**Serves 12-14**

# Rancher's Marinated Chicken Livers

*Chickens and roosters roam freely at the Farm.*

*For a change in main courses, here's a tasty, unique and simple way to serve chicken livers. To serve this dish at its best, don't overcook the livers.*

- 1 cup sherry, sweet
- 1½ teaspoons tarragon
- salt and pepper to taste
- 1½ pounds chicken livers

- 1 onion, sliced
- ½ green pepper, sliced
- 2 tablespoons vegetable oil
- 2 teaspoons French-style mustard

In a bowl, combine sherry, tarragon, salt and pepper. Pour over chicken livers in a shallow baking dish. Marinate at room temperature for 2 hours.

In a skillet, saute onion and pepper in oil until tender. Remove chicken livers from marinade with a slotted spoon and add them to onions in the skillet. Reserve marinade. Saute livers until brown on all sides, turning often. Add mustard to reserved marinade and blend thoroughly. Pour marinade over livers and simmer uncovered for 5 minutes. Remove chicken livers to a warm serving platter and continue simmering sauce for 5 additional minutes. Pour over livers. Serve on a bed of steamed rice or cooked noodles.

**Serves 4**

# Chicken A La Boysenberry

*An unusual combination of ingredients makes for an equally unusual flavor sensation. Try it.*

- 4 whole chicken breasts, split, boned and skinned
- ¾ cup butter
- salt, freshly ground pepper and nutmeg to taste
- 8 thin slices ham
- ¼ pound chicken livers, quartered
- 2 cups sliced fresh mushrooms
- 1 tablespoon lemon juice
- ½ cup minced onion
- 2⅓ cups chicken broth
- 1 cup medium dry Madeira wine
- ⅔ cup Knott's Boysenberry Preserves
- ¼ cup cornstarch
- 4 cups cooked wild rice
- ¼ cup minced parsley

Lightly brown chicken breasts in ¼ cup of the butter and continue sauteing until thoroughly cooked or about 10 minutes. Season with salt, pepper and nutmeg. Set aside and keep warm. Saute ham in pan juices; set aside with chicken. Cook chicken livers until lightly browned, stirring often; set aside. Heat ¼ cup butter in same pan. Add mushrooms, stir until shiny, then sprinkle with lemon juice. Gently cook for 2 minutes; add to chicken. Heat remaining butter in same pan; add onion and cook until tender. Blend in chicken livers, 2 cups of the chicken broth, the Madeira wine and preserves. Cook and stir 5 minutes to blend flavors. Season with additional salt, pepper and nutmeg. Blend cornstarch into remaining ⅓ cup chicken broth. Add to sauce; cook and stir until thickened and smooth.

For each serving arrange chicken and mushrooms on ham slice on bed of rice. Top with sauce and garnish with parsley.

Serves 8

*Board a stagecoach and get ready to roll.*

# Branding Iron Meatballs

*Shish kebab your hamburger! The sweet-and-sour sauce sparks up the flavor of plain old ground beef.*

SAUCE:
- ½ onion, chopped
- 2 tablespoons vegetable oil
- 1 8-ounce can tomato sauce
- 8 ounces dry red wine (or water)
- ¼ cup cider vinegar
- ¼ cup Knott's Orange Honey
- 1 teaspoon salt
- 1 teaspoon Worcestershire sauce
- ½ teaspoon tabasco

Saute onion in oil until soft. Add remaining ingredients to saucepan with onions and bring to a boil. Simmer for 5 to 10 minutes. Pour into a large glass pan and cool.

MEATBALLS:
- 2 pounds ground beef
- 2 eggs
- 1 onion, grated
- ¼ to ½ cup cracker crumbs (or bread crumbs)
- 2 garlic cloves, minced
- salt and pepper to taste

green or red pepper, onion or tomato
sesame seeds

Blend ground beef with eggs, onion, crumbs, garlic and salt and pepper so it will shape into firm ball. Make 1½ inch diameter balls and carefully put two on a small wooden skewer with a chunk of green or red pepper, onion or tomato, in between balls. Cover ends of wooden skewers with aluminum foil to prevent burning.

Marinate meatballs in cooled sauce for 1 hour or more, turning occasionally. Broil on foil-covered broiler pan for 5 minutes or until brown and turn being careful not to break meatballs. Sprinkle with sesame seeds and broil an additional 5 minutes. Serve on a bed of plain rice.

**Yields 26 meatballs**

# Railroad Tie Riblets

*Here's a fancy way to dress up an inexpensive cut of meat. Test it as an hors d'oeuvre, and you'll then want to feature it later as a main course.*

- 2 pounds lamb riblets
- 1 6-ounce jar Knott's Apricot & Pineapple Preserves
- ½ cup soy sauce
- 1½ tablespoons lemon juice
- 1 teaspoon sweet basil, crushed
- ½ teaspoon dry mustard

Heat oven to 375°. Place riblets in broiler pan or baking dish and cook for 15 minutes. Pour off fat and return to oven for 5 minutes more. Combine remaining ingredients and heat just to boiling in a saucepan. Coat each riblet with marinade and return to oven for 10 minutes. Rotate riblets and bake another 10 minutes.

Marinade can be made in advance and stored in refrigerator until ready to use. Spareribs can be substituted for lamb riblets.

**Serves 4**

*Built in 1881, the Calico Railway can still give you a good time.*

# Barber Shop Beef Fondue

For fun get-togethers, this everyone-do-it-yourself dish is entertaining and novel. Calorie watchers can substitute boiling beef stock for the oil.

  2 **pounds top sirloin**
  ¼ **cup soy sauce**
  ½ **teaspoon garlic powder**
  ¼ **teaspoon dry mustard**

Cut meat into bite-size cubes and discard any tough membranes or fat. Place in a shallow baking dish. Combine remaining ingredients and mix thoroughly. Pour over meat and refrigerate until ready to serve. When ready to serve, remove meat from marinade and place on a serving platter.

  2 **cups vegetable oil**

    **Knott's Steakhouse Meat Relish**
    **Knott's Thousand Island Dressing**
    **scallions, chopped**
    **mushrooms, chopped**

*Handsome Brady and Whiskey Bill set a spell and watch the crowds.*

In a small saucepan, heat oil to almost boiling. Place saucepan on a portable burner at the table to keep oil hot. Have each guest skewer a piece of meat on a long bamboo stick and plunge into hot oil. The meat will cook quickly. Pass individual bowls of sauces and dressings for dipping.

**Serves 4-6**

# Butterfield Stage Spareribs

*Don't let these ingredients "hold you up" from trying this recipe. They gang-up nicely with just the right amount of zest.*

**2 pounds spareribs**

Cut rack into individual ribs and render off the fat by placing in a 375° oven for 15 minutes. Pour off all the fat.

SAUCE:
- ¼ **cup Knott's All-Purpose Dressing**
- 1 **teaspoon chili powder**
- 1 **teaspoon paprika**
- 1 **teaspoon salt**
- 2 **tablespoons Knott's Clover Honey**
- ¼ **cup catsup**
- ¼ **cup vinegar**

In a saucepan, combine all sauce ingredients and cook over low heat for 5 minutes. Roll each rib in the sauce to coat. Bake in 350° oven for 35 minutes, turning every 10 to 15 minutes. (If the ribs are very thick, they may take an additional 10 minutes.)

**Serves 4-5**

*Watch out for masked bandits while riding the Butterfield Stagecoach.*

# Old Timer's Stuffed Veal

Here's a clever way to serve this seldom-used economical cut of meat. The next time you see a veal breast in your butcher's case, be adventurous and try it this way.

- 2 garlic cloves, minced
- 2 onions, chopped
- ½ green pepper, chopped
- 4 tablespoons butter
- 8 carrots, grated
- 4 stalks celery, grated
- 1 zucchini, grated
- 4 tablespoons oatmeal
- 4 tablespoons flour
- 2 tablespoons dry red wine

- 1 6-pound veal breast
- 1 onion, sliced
- 2 garlic cloves, minced
- ¼ green pepper, sliced
- 8 carrots, whole
- 8 mushrooms, halved or quartered
- 1 teaspoon sweet basil
- 1 teaspoon tarragon
- 1 cup dry red or white wine
- 1 tablespoon tomato paste

In a large skillet, saute garlic, onions and green pepper in butter until soft. Add carrots, celery and zucchini and mix with a wooden spoon and simmer for 5 minutes. Add oatmeal, flour and wine and blend thoroughly. Spoon into pocket of veal breast and seal opening with needle and thread.

In a large roasting pan, place half of onion, garlic and green pepper and place stuffed veal breast on top. Surround with carrots and mushrooms. Sprinkle with basil, tarragon and remaining onion, garlic and green pepper. Mix wine with tomato paste and pour over veal breast. Add more liquid if sauce reduces too rapidly. Cover and roast in preheated 375° oven for 2 to 3 hours or until tender.

**Serves 6-8**

# Prospector's Pork Tenderloin

*The spiced sauce takes a pork tenderloin into the gourmet class. Couple this with the "Calico Can-Can Casserole" in this section.*

- ½ cup red wine
- ½ cup water
- 1 onion, peeled and sliced
- 2 tablespoons shallots, chopped (or scallions)
- ½ teaspoon ground cinnamon
- 1 small bay leaf
- 1 whole clove
- 3 sprigs parsley
- ⅛ teaspoon salt
- pepper
- 2 pounds pork tenderloin, ½-inch slices

- 3 tablespoons butter and oil
- 2 tablespoons flour
- ½ cup chicken stock
- 2 tablespoons brandy

In a bowl, combine wine, water, onion, shallots, cinnamon, bay leaf, clove, parsley, thyme, salt and pepper. Arrange meat slices in one layer in a shallow dish and pour marinade over, turning to moisten. Marinate 2 hours turning once.

Remove steaks from marinade and reserve marinade. Heat butter and oil in a large skillet and brown steaks for 2 or 3 minutes on each side. Transfer to baking dish and set aside.

Add flour to fat in skillet and cook on low heat, mixing with wooden spoon until flour is lightly browned. Pour in strained marinade, chicken stock and brandy. Stir constantly with wire whisk and bring to a boil stirring constantly until sauce is smooth and slightly thickened. Taste for seasoning. Pour sauce over steaks and bake for 5 minutes.

**Serves 6-8**

# Mother Lode Country Pastry

*Hold on tight during your exciting ride through the Mother Lode Country.*

*It's not a cake, or a bread, or a roll, or a streudel. It's really all of them rolled up into one — and filled with chocolate.*

- 1 cup plus 2 tablespoons flour
- 2 tablespoons sugar
- ½ teaspoon salt
- 2 tablespoons butter
- 1 egg
- 2 tablespoons sour cream
- ½ teaspoon grated lemon rind
- 1 package yeast (1½ teaspoons)
- 1 tablespoon lukewarm milk

- 2 cups instant cocoa
- ¼ cup water
- 1 cup walnuts, chopped
- 1 cup raisins

In a bowl, combine flour, sugar and salt. Add butter and combine until crumbly. Add egg and sour cream and lemon rind. In a small bowl, combine yeast and milk. When dissolved, add yeast to flour mixture and beat. Let rise covered in a warm place for about 2 hours or until double in bulk. Punch down and roll out on lightly floured board into a 12-inch circle. Brush dough with melted butter.

In a bowl, combine cocoa with water and add nuts and raisins and spread mixture over dough leaving a 1-inch border all around. Roll up jelly-roll fashion and form a crescent. Transfer to buttered cookie sheet, brush with melted butter and let rise covered for 45 minutes or until double in bulk. Bake in 375° oven for 20 minutes or until golden brown. Let cool on wire rack. Sprinkle with powdered sugar.

# Log Ride Chocolate Roll

*Thrilling to serve and eat, this exciting new dessert offers a challenge to prepare. Don't be discouraged if your first attempt isn't perfect — your second one will be worth the effort.*

- 7 **eggs, separated**
- ¾ **cup sugar**
- 7 **ounces dark German sweet chocolate, chunked**
- 3 **tablespoons coffee (liquid)**
- 3 **tablespoons Kahlua coffee liqueur bitter cocoa**
- 1 **12-ounce jar Knott's Bing Cherry or Red Cherry Preserves**

- 1 **pint whipping cream**
- 1 **tablespoon powdered sugar**
- ¼ **teaspoon vanilla**

Beat egg yolks until thick and fluffy. Add sugar, a ¼ cup at a time, and continue to beat until thick and forms a wide ribbon. Combine chocolate, coffee and Kahlua in a saucepan and melt chocolate over low heat, stirring constantly. Remove from heat and allow to cool, then add to egg yolk mixture. Beat egg whites until they form stiff peaks and gently fold into chocolate mixture.

Line a greased cookie sheet with wax paper and pour on batter. Bake in preheated 375° oven for 17 minutes.

Remove from oven and cover with 3 paper towels (the center towel should be barely damp). Allow to cool for 20 minutes then remove paper towels. Dust chocolate roll with sifted cocoa. Carefully turn out roll onto overlapping wax paper. Peel off wax paper adhering to bottom then evenly spread preserves on roll.

Combine cream, sugar and vanilla and whip until stiff. Spread cream on preserves evenly. Roll up, jelly roll style, very carefully, onto serving platter. Cracks may occur but will not ruin roll. Dust top with cocoa and serve or refrigerate until ready to use.

**Serves 6-8**

*The Log Ride is one of the most popular and exciting adventures.*

# School House Apple Pie

See how your grandparents learned readin', writin' and 'rithmetic in the Little Red Schoolhouse.

*The crunchy crumb topping is even better than the usual top crust in this spiced apple pie.*

- 1 **10-inch pie shell**\* (see recipe for "Flapper Fruity Tarts" in Roaring 20's section)
- ½ **cup sugar**
- 1 **teaspoon cinnamon**
- ¼ **teaspoon allspice**
- ¼ **teaspoon nutmeg**
- 1 **tablespoon flour**
- 6 **cups peeled, cored and sliced green apples**
- 1 **tablespoon lemon juice**
- 2 **tablespoons butter**
  **Crumb Topping** (recipe below)

Combine sugar, cinnamon, allspice, nutmeg and flour in a large mixing bowl. Add apples, lemon juice and toss gently. Fill partially baked pie shell and dot with butter. Cover apples with crumb topping.

CRUMB TOPPING:
- ½ **cup sugar**
- ¾ **cup flour**
- ⅓ **cup butter**

Mix sugar with flour and cut in butter until crumbly.

Bake pie in preheated 400° oven for 40 minutes or until apples are cooked.

\*Brush unbaked pie shell with 3 tablespoons Knott's Apricot Preserves.

# School Marm Jam Jems

*Betcha can't eat just one of these bite-sized beauties. After your first test, you'll double this recipe to fully satisfy all your dessert lovers.*

- 1 cup vegetable shortening
- 1 cup brown sugar
- 2 egg yolks
- 1 teaspoon vanilla
- ½ teaspoon salt
- 2 cups flour
- 2 egg whites
- 1 cup chopped walnuts
- Assorted Knott's preserves

Cream shortening and brown sugar together until fluffy. Add egg yolks and vanilla and continue mixing. Add sifted flour and salt and mix until thoroughly blended. Take out of bowl and work into a ball with hands. Can be refrigerated or frozen at this point by wrapping dough in plastic wrap.

Roll dough into ¾" balls and dip into egg whites and roll in chopped nuts. Place cookies on greased cookie sheet and gently press in the center of each cookie with your finger or a thimble. Bake in a preheated 350° oven for 10 minutes. Press down the indentation again as in baking the cookies will rise. Continue baking for 5 more minutes or until golden brown. When cool or ready to serve, drop a quarter of a teaspoon of selected Knott's preserves in the center of each cookie.

**Yields 3½ dozen**

*Dressed up like yesteryear, a school marm still "teaches" history like it really was a century ago.*

*Mexican Bouillabaisse, Masa Harina Bread, Albondigas, Green Pepper Jelly*

*Enchiladas* con Pollo Real, Fiesta Guisada

# FIESTA VILLAGE™

An oasis of early Latin culture has been magically transformed from Old Mexico by way of Early Spanish California to right here and now. Strolling mariachis and colorful flamenco dancers lead you on a sparkling walk from the central Plaza through open stall markets and hand-decorated buildings, the Animal Farm, past the 1896 Dentzel Merry-Go-Round, weekend fireworks, beside the Bell Wall of Happiness, Fiesta Island, the bandstand and lake, with lovely fuchsias and bougainvilleas at every turn, and historic recreations of California's 21 famous Franciscan missions along El Camino Real (The King's Highway) which extended from San Diego in the south to Sonoma in the north. A quiet slice of South-of-the-Border charm, this Old Time Adventure also offers fun and excitement for gay caballeros and their saucy senoritas in the daring "Mexican Whip," "Fiesta Wheel" and "Happy Sombrero." In this section, our recipes are Mexican in flavor, with the spice, zest and liveliness associated with its people. From an enchilada to a flan, the recipes are fun to prepare, serve, talk about, and eat.

# Mexican Bouillabaisse

*It's really a Mexican bouillabaisse, without saffron but with cilantro. And the Madeira makes the other flavor difference.*

- 4 tablespoons olive oil
- 2 onions, sliced
- ½ green pepper, chopped
- 1 garlic clove, minced
- 1 28-ounce can tomatoes, chunked and drained
- ½ teaspoon oregano, crushed
- 1 bay leaf
- 1 teaspoon salt
- ¼ teaspoon pepper
- 2 potatoes, peeled and sliced
- 4 cups fish stock, water or white wine
- 3 pounds chowder fish, cut in large chunks
- 1 tablespoon cilantro, fresh, chopped
- 2 tablespoons parsley, fresh, chopped
- 1 cup Madeira

In a large Dutch oven, heat oil and saute onions, green pepper and garlic until golden. Add tomatoes, oregano, bay leaf, salt and pepper and cook for 5 minutes, stirring with a wooden spoon. Add potatoes, stock, and cilantro and bring to a boil. Simmer covered for 15 to 20 minutes or until potatoes are tender to fork. Add fish and cook an additional 10 minutes or until fish is firm.

Just before serving add parsley and Madeira and cook over medium heat uncovered for 5 minutes. Ladle into individual soup bowls and serve.

Serves 8-10

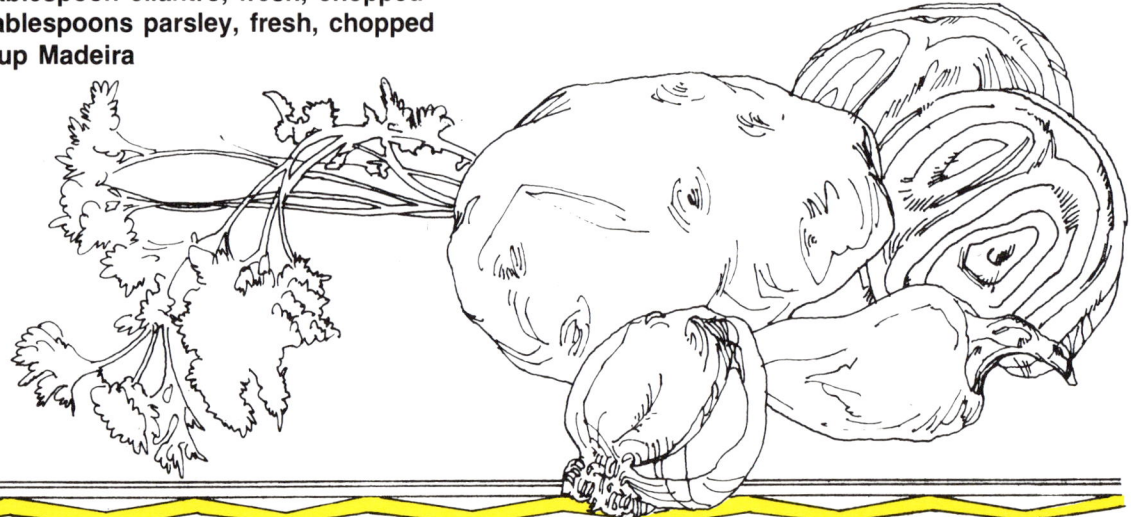

# Cantina Albondigas
## (MEATBALL SOUP)

*This new version of the traditional Mexican meatball soup has almost everything in it including chili powder. It also uses fresh mint, cumin, oregano and cilantro to capture the authentic Mexican taste.*

**Meatballs:** (Albondigas)
- 1 pound ground beef or half beef and half pork
- ½ onion, chopped or grated
- 1 tablespoon fresh cilantro (or ¼ teaspoon coriander)
- ½ teaspoon oregano, crushed
- 1 egg
- 2 tablespoons rice, uncooked
- ¼ cup parsley, chopped
- 1 teaspoon salt
- 2 tablespoons breadcrumbs or corn meal

Mix above ingredients together, blending well. Shape into balls and set aside. (Can be used for hors d'oeuvres or filling for tortillas.)

**Soup:** (Caldo)
- 8 cups beef stock
- 4 soup bones (at least 1 marrow bone)
- ½ head cabbage, sliced
- 2 large onions, sliced
- 1 28-ounce can tomatoes, quartered, with liquid
- 15 sprigs cilantro
- 1 sprig fresh mint, chopped (or 1 teaspoon dried mint)
- 3 garlic cloves, minced
- 1 teaspoon chili powder
- ½ teaspoon cumin
- 5 carrots, peeled and chopped
- 2 celery stalks, chopped
- ½ can (7½ ounces) garbanzo beans, drained
- 1 teaspoon salt
- ¼ teaspoon pepper

In a large pot, place stock and bones and bring to a boil then skim off top. Add remaining ingredients; reduce heat and simmer partially covered for 1 hour or until vegetables are soft. Add meatballs and simmer an additional 30 minutes.

Serve with hot tortillas or the Masa Harina bread recipe found in this section. Garnish with chopped cilantro.

**Serves 8**

# Sopa De Ajo
## (GARLIC SOUP)

El Camino Real – The King's Highway.

*Hearty country folk know the health-aid values of garlic. So don't be afraid of overcooking as the longer the stock simmers the more full-bodied the flavor.*

- 2 quarts water
- 24 cloves of garlic
- 1 sprig of parsley
- 1 sprig of thyme
- 2 cloves
-   pinch of sage
-   pinch of pepper
- 4 teaspoons salt

GARNISH:
- 6-8 egg yolks (whole)
-   toast rounds
- ½ pound jack cheese, grated

In a large pot combine all ingredients (except garnish) and boil rapidly for 30 to 45 minutes. This will reduce down to a rich stock.

To serve, place oven-proof coffee cups or soup bowls on a cookie sheet, put one raw egg yolk in each cup, and strain hot soup into cups. Float a round of lightly toasted bread on top of each cup and sprinkle generously with jack cheese. Put into oven or under broiler until cheese melts, and serve at once.

**Serves 6-8**

# Ceviche Ensalada

*The fish in this recipe is not uncooked, it's cured by the marinating in the lemon or lime juice. A popular Mexican delicacy, this salad is both healthful and low in calories.*

**1 pound halibut or red snapper**
**1 cup lemon or lime juice**

**2 tomatoes, peeled\*, seeded and diced**
**1 onion, chopped**
**1 clove garlic, minced**
**3 tablespoons cilantro (or substitute ¼ teaspoon cumin and ¼ teaspoon thyme)**
**salt and pepper**

Wash fish and cut in ½-inch cubes. Place in a glass bowl with lemon or lime juice for 3 hours or more. Mix with a wooden spoon several times.

Mix tomatoes, onion, garlic and cilantro with marinated fish and toss. Add salt and pepper to taste.

Serve on a bed of lettuce or fill 6 avocado halves placed on a bed of lettuce.

\*Plunge tomatoes into boiling water for 30 seconds, remove with a slotted spoon and peel.

**Serves 6**

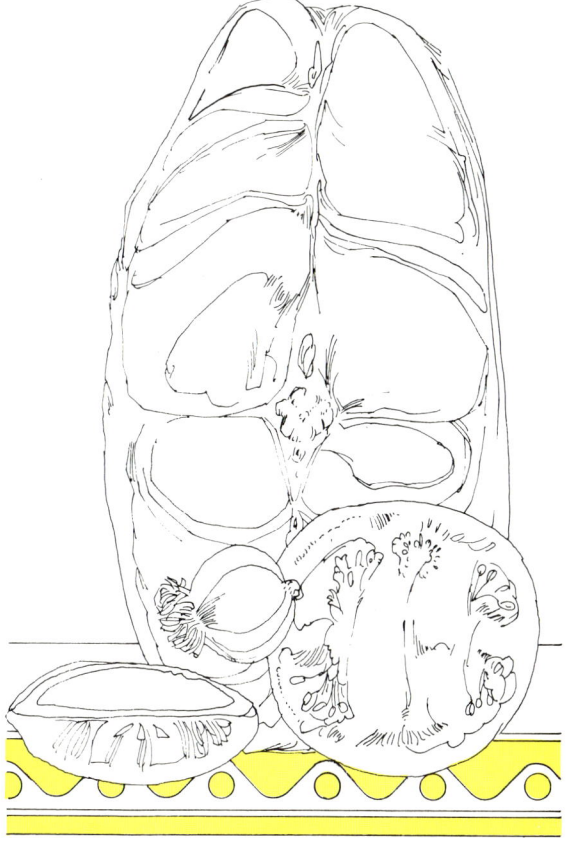

# Jicama And Cheese Salad

Watching the passing parade of visitors is this curious goat.

*Jicama (pronounced with an h) is a sweet-tasting Central American vegetable that has almost no calories but lots of food value. Usually eaten sliced with just lemon or lime juice, our variation makes it a full salad instead of a snack.*

- 1 cup jicama, peeled and julienne
- 1 cup jack cheese, julienne
- ¼ cup pimiento, sliced

- ¼ cup lemon juice
- ⅓ cup vegetable oil
- ¼ teaspoon chili powder
- ½ teaspoon grated onion
- ¼ teaspoon oregano, crushed

Prepare jicama, jack cheese and pimientos and set aside in a large bowl.

In a separate bowl combine remaining ingredients and mix thoroughly. Pour this dressing over jicama and cheese mixture and toss well. Let stand for 15 minutes before serving, then mound on a bed of Bibb lettuce.

**Serves 4**

# El Pueblo Guacamole

Here's a novel variation of the familiar guacamole. Instead of mashing or pureeing the avocado, our chopped-in-chunks method gives a great new texture and lets you appreciate the avocado flavor.

- 1 avocado, chopped in chunks
- ½ tomato, chopped
- ½ onion, chopped
- 1 tablespoon fresh cilantro, chopped
- 1 tablespoon lemon juice
- ⅛ teaspoon chili powder
- salt and pepper to taste

- 1 tomato
- lettuce for garnish

In a large bowl, combine avocado, tomato and onion. Add cilantro, lemon juice, chili powder, salt and pepper and gently toss with wooden spoon. Place avocado seed in center of avocado mixture which is now guacamole, cover and refrigerate.

When ready to serve, place lettuce leaves on a serving plate, cut tomato in eighths but do not cut completely through and place in center of lettuce leaves. Spread tomato sections like a flower and spoon on guacamole.

**Serves 4**

*A fine example of early Spanish California architecture.*

# Green Pepper Jelly

*Fun for everyone in Fiesta Village.*

*Jalapeno, which means green pepper, as a jelly, is becoming more popular here in the U.S. Serve as an hors d'oeuvre spread on cream cheese and wafer-thin brown bread, or even top slices of bologna with it, rolled and served on a toothpick. Or, let your imagination create your own original use for this spicy, versatile jelly.*

- 3 long green chili peppers
- 1 green bell pepper
- 1½ cups cider vinegar
- 5 cups sugar
- ½ teaspoon cayenne pepper
- ½ bottle (3 ounces) liquid pectin

Wash, seed and chop chili peppers and bell pepper. In a blender, put ½ cup vinegar, chilies and green pepper and puree. In a Dutch oven, mix sugar, cayenne pepper, peppers and remaining vinegar. Bring to a boil slowly, stirring constantly. Boil 2 minutes. Remove from heat, skim foam with metal spoon. Stir in pectin and mix well. Ladle into hot, sterilized jars and seal immediately.

**Yields 3 pints or 6 cups**

# Plaza Pimientos

*Mostly we think of pimientos as something that adds color and subtle flavor to many dishes. But let it stand on its own, served simply on a bed of lettuce and discover this new super salad.*

 4  **red or green bell peppers**
⅓ **cup Knott's Italian Dressing**

Preheat oven to 375°. Lay a sheet of foil on lower rack. Place peppers on upper-middle rack. Bake 15 minutes or until top skin of peppers starts to brown or skin bubbles away from meat of peppers. Turn peppers and continue baking for 15 minutes longer or until skin of peppers can be peeled away easily. Place hot peppers on a plate and carefully peel. Discard skin, stem and seeds, reserving juices that drain from inside of peppers. Cut peppers in thirds and place in a glass bowl. Pour reserved liquid over peppers and dressing. Cover and refrigerate.

Serve as a salad on a bed of lettuce or sliced as a garnish.

*Graceful archways welcome you to Fiesta Village.*

# Masa Harina Bread

Ground corn is an important food staple South of the Border.

It tastes and smells just like tortillas, but it has the advantage of being a bread. Try it toasted for breakfast, or serve it with the "Queso Chili Casserole" in this section.

2½ cups flour
1 package dry yeast
1 tablespoon sugar
2 teaspoons salt
2 cups warm water
2 cups masa harina
2 tablespoons corn meal

In a large mixer bowl combine flour, yeast, sugar and salt. Add water and beat at low speed of electric mixer for 1 minute. Beat at high speed for 3 minutes. Add masa harina and mix thoroughly. Turn out onto floured board and knead gently for 5 minutes. Shape into a ball, place in a greased bowl and grease top. Cover and let rise in a warm place for 1½ hours or until double in bulk. Punch down, and divide in half. Cover and let rise 10 minutes. Shape into two loaves and place on a cookie sheet which has been oiled and sprinkled with corn meal. Cover with a kitchen towel and let rise in warm place until double in size or about 45 minutes.

Brush tops with milk and bake in preheated 375° oven for 25 to 30 minutes. Remove from loaf pans and cool on rack.

**Yields 2 loaves**

# Happy Sombrero Sopaipillas
## (FRIED BISCUITS)

*These little triangle biscuits are so good served warm with honey. Great with any meal, they also make a delicious in-between snack.*

- 2 cups flour
- 2 teaspoons baking powder
- 1 teaspoon salt
- 2 tablespoons shortening or margarine
- ½ cup lukewarm water

**Knott's Clover Honey**

In a large mixing bowl, sift together flour, baking powder and salt. Add shortening and blend until crumbly. Add water and mix thoroughly. Turn out on a floured board and knead gently for 2 minutes. Roll out thin and cut into triangles. Deep fry three triangles at a time at 400°, turning once, until golden brown on all sides. Remove with slotted spoon and drain on paper towels. Serve while still warm with honey, with a main course.

**Yields 24**

*Round and round you go, happily.*

# Aztec Squash

*Fiesta Village offers a romantic setting of Latin culture.*

This ancient and most common of squash becomes an uncommon treat when adding our Knott's Steakhouse Meat Relish. This colorful vegetable also decorates your dinner plate.

- 1½ **pounds yellow crookneck squash or zucchini**
- 2 **tablespoons margarine or butter**
- ⅔ **cup Knott's Steakhouse Meat Relish**

Slice squash in ½ inch slices and steam until tender but still firm. (If you cannot steam vegetables, boil in one cup salted water.) Do not overcook. Drain and add margarine to squash and cook only until margarine melts. Add meat relish and warm thoroughly.

**Serves 4**

# Queso Chili Casserole

For that occasional meatless lunch or dinner, this tasty but not spicy Mexican-inspired casserole will win "Oles." Don't skimp on the cheeses, and be sure to remove all seeds from the chilies.

- 1 7-ounce can green chilies
- 1 pound sharp cheddar cheese, grated
- 1 pound jack cheese, grated (reserve some for topping)
- 2 large cans evaporated milk
- 4 eggs, slightly beaten
- ½ cup corn meal
- 1 teaspoon salt
- 1 teaspoon Worcestershire sauce
- 1 medium tomato, sliced

Split chilies and wash out seeds. Layer chilies and cheeses in a casserole. Combine milk, eggs, corn meal, salt and Worcestershire sauce. Pour into casserole with chili mixture and bake 30 minutes at 350°. Remove from oven, add reserved jack cheese and garnish with sliced tomatoes. Bake 15 minutes more.

**Serves 6-8**

*Singing and dancing fill the air in Fiesta Village.*

# Pescado A La Pacifica

*Spice up your next fish entree with this "super sauce." Pass around hot tortillas, spoon on some of the sauce and enjoy them along with this fish.*

- 2 tablespoons olive oil
- 1 onion, chopped
- 3 garlic cloves, minced
- 1 28-ounce can tomatoes, drained and chopped
- 4 tablespoons parsley, chopped
- 1 tablespoon lemon juice (or vinegar)
- 1 teaspoon salt
- 1 bay leaf
- ¼ teaspoon thyme
- ¼ teaspoon marjoram
- ¼ teaspoon oregano
- 1 teaspoon sugar
- ¼ cup wine
- 1 4-ounce can green chili, chopped
- 2 teaspoons capers

- 1 pound red snapper or tutuava (6 pieces)
  salt and pepper
- 2 tablespoons olive oil

In a large skillet heat oil and saute onion and garlic until golden. Add tomatoes, parsley, lemon juice, salt, bay leaf, thyme, marjoram, oregano, sugar, wine, chili and capers. Simmer for 5 to 10 minutes. Set aside.

Sprinkle fish with salt and pepper. Saute in hot oil for one minute on each side and place in a large baking dish. Pour sauce over fish and bake in preheated 300° oven for 20 to 30 minutes until fish is tender.

Place individual portions of fish on each plate, place rice to side of fish and spoon additional sauce on rice.

**Serves 6**

# Enchiladas Con Pollo

*These chicken enchiladas are outstandingly delicious and different. Combining raisins, almonds and olives with the chicken and cheese gives enchiladas a whole new taste.*

- ½ cup apple juice
- ¼ cup raisins
- 2 cups chicken, cooked and diced
- ½ cup onion, minced
- ⅓ cup pitted ripe olives, sliced
- ⅓ cup almonds, blanched and slivered
- 2¼ cup sauce (recipe follows)
- 12 corn tortillas
- 1 cup Jack cheese, grated

Plump raisins in apple juice in the refrigerator for 1 hour. Drain. In a bowl, mix together raisins, chicken, onions, olives, almonds and ¼ cup sauce. Heat tortillas one at a time on a hot griddle or skillet to soften. Do not allow the tortillas to get crisp. Dip into sauce and fill each tortilla with 2 or 3 tablespoons filling and roll up. Spoon some sauce on the bottom of a 9" x 13" baking dish and place rolled tortillas in dish seam side down. Spoon on sauce and sprinkle with cheese. Bake in a preheated 350° oven for 20 minutes or until cheese bubbles.

**Yields 12 enchiladas**

SAUCE:
- 1½ onions, minced
- 3 tablespoons oil
- 3 garlic cloves, crushed
- 3 7-ounce bottles taco sauce
- 2¼ cups chicken stock
- ½ teaspoon cumin, ground
- ½ teaspoon oregano
- ½ teaspoon salt

Saute onion and garlic in oil until tender. Add remaining ingredients and simmer covered for 30 minutes, stirring occasionally.

**Yields 6 cups**

# Fiesta Guisado

*Geese greet visitors to their farmyard home.*

*Feature this festive fare for your next family fiesta. Basically a stew, the unique flavors add gaiety to a popular repast.*

- ¼ cup oil
- 2 onions, sliced
- 3 cloves garlic, minced
- ½ green pepper, diced
- 4 pounds round or shoulder roast, 1-inch strips
- 2 teaspoons oregano, crushed
- 1 teaspoon cumin, ground
- 3 tablespoons fresh cilantro, chopped or 1 teaspoon coriander
- 1½ teaspoons salt
- pepper to taste
- 1 28-ounce can whole tomatoes, chopped
- 2 fresh California green chilies, diced or 1 4-ounce can green chilies

In a Dutch oven, heat oil and saute onions, garlic and green pepper until soft. Add meat in small amounts and brown on all sides, mixing with a wooden spoon. Stir in oregano, cumin, cilantro, salt and pepper. Add tomatoes including liquid and chilies. Simmer partially covered until meat is tender or about 1½ to 2 hours.

Serve with either flour or corn tortillas.

**Serves 8**

# Fiesta Wheels Tostadas

*This open-faced taco can be made with or without meat and even with any leftover chicken or turkey. The taco sauce refrigerates well for use in other Mexican recipes.*

- 6 tortillas
- ¼ cup oil
- 1 17-ounce can refried beans
- 1 cup Taco Sauce (recipe below)
- shredded lettuce
- 1 pound leftover meat or chicken
- guacamole (see "El Pueblo Guacamole" recipe in this section)
- cheddar cheese, grated

In a skillet, fry each tortilla in oil until crisp. Drain on paper towels. Place on individual plates. Spoon on beans, taco sauce, lettuce, chunks of meat or chicken (leftover meat should be placed under broiler for a few minutes to heat), guacamole, cheese and more taco sauce.

**Serves 6**

TACO SAUCE:
- ⅓ cup oil
- 1½ teaspoons oregano, crumbled
- 1 pound tomatoes, peeled and chopped fine
- 1 bunch cilantro, chopped
- 3 green onions, minced
- 2 4-ounce cans green chilies, drained and chopped
- ½ teaspoon salt

Combine oil and oregano, then add tomatoes, cilantro, onions, chilies and salt. Store in refrigerator.

**Yields 1 quart**

# Taquitos Verdes

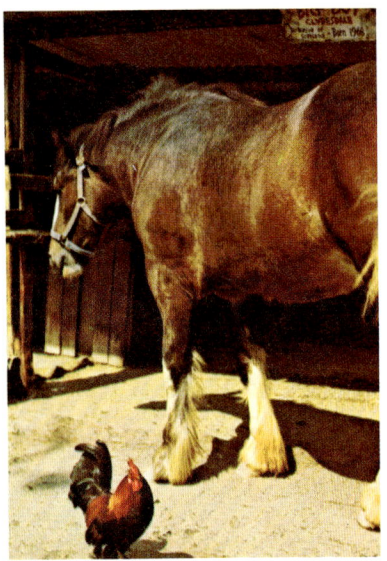

Even the rooster isn't afraid of "Big Boy," the Clydesdale on the Farm.

The trick in keeping your tortillas pliable so that they can be rolled is carefully heating them in a skillet for just a few seconds. It's easy once you've tried it. Because the taquito is plain by itself, the avocado sauce is a necessary part of this recipe. Taquitos would go great with the soups in this section.

1 cup leftover roast beef or chicken
12 corn tortillas
1 onion, chopped

avocado sauce

In a large skillet or griddle, heat tortillas, to soften, one at a time. Place strips of meat or chicken and onions lengthwise on one end of tortilla, spoon on 1 teaspoon sauce and roll up. Close final overlapping flap with a toothpick broken in half. Place on plate, cover with foil and refrigerate.

When ready to serve, fry in hot oil in a large skillet, turning to brown evenly. Drain on paper towel. Serve with green salsa or avocado sauce and top with a dollop of sour cream if desired.

**Serves 6**

AVOCADO SAUCE:
1 avocado
1 teaspoon lemon juice
½ teaspoon salt
⅛ teaspoon chili powder
2 tablespoons onion, grated

Combine all ingredients and mash with fork or potato masher. Refrigerate covered until ready to use.

**Yields 1 cup**

# Castanets Cheese Casserole

*The layering of the mild green chilies blends nicely with the jack cheese and sour cream to create a new taste treat. It's easy to make and economical to serve.*

- 3 scallions
- 1 pint sour cream
- 1 pound jack cheese, grated
- 1 4-ounce can mild green cut chili
- ¾ cup chicken broth

- 12 corn tortillas, quartered
- ¼ pound margarine, melted

Slice scallions thin and set aside green slices. In a bowl, place white part of scallions, sour cream, ¾ pound cheese, chilies and broth and mix well.

Soften tortillas in melted margarine and place half of the tortillas in a deep baking dish or casserole. Pour half the cheese mixture over the tortillas. Layer with four of the quartered tortillas and pour in remaining cheese mixture. Place remaining tortilla quarters evenly on mixture and top with remaining ¼ pound cheese. Sprinkle top with reserved green scallion slices. Place in 325° oven for 35 minutes.

**Serves 6-8**

# Flamenco Flan

Flamenco dancers at their colorful best.

*The cashew butter sauce, instead of the customary caramel, makes this an entirely new dessert while retaining the traditional Mexican custard.*

1 14-ounce can sweetened condensed milk
1 13-ounce can evaporated milk
1 cup milk
1 teaspoon vanilla
5 eggs

**Cashew Butter Sauce** (recipe below)
¼ **cup cashew nuts, chopped**

Combine all ingredients except sauce and nuts in a blender and blend thoroughly. Pour into a baking dish or individual custard cups and set in a water bath. Bake in a preheated 350° oven for one hour or until knife comes out clean. Remove from water bath and set aside to cool. Spoon sauce on each serving and sprinkle chopped nuts on top.

CASHEW BUTTER SAUCE:
⅓ cup Knott's Cashew Butter
⅓ cup milk
3 tablespoons brown sugar

Combine all ingredients in a saucepan and place over low heat, mixing constantly until all ingredients are blended and cashew butter has melted. (Should you wish to prepare this sauce in advance, pour into a thermos which has been rinsed in warm water and close tightly. Sauce will stay warm until ready to use.)

**Serves 8**

# Tamales Dulces
## (SWEET TAMALES)

*There are very few Mexican desserts, and sweet tamales is one of them. Our new variation of this popular treat is a delightful ending to any meal.*

- 20 corn husks, soaked in hot water for 1 hour
- 2 cups masa harina, soaked in 1½ cups water
- ⅔ cup vegetable shortening
- 1 cup sugar
- 4 teaspoons baking powder
- ½ teaspoon salt
- 1 7-ounce can pineapple chunks, drained and cut in pieces

Cream shortening with sugar until light and fluffy. Add soaked masa harina, baking powder and salt and beat until a little batter floats in a glass of cold water. Fold in pineapple.

Drain corn husks. Place a spoonful of the pineapple batter in the center of each corn husk. Roll up and fold ends over and steam in a colander over water until light and fluffy — about 20 to 30 minutes.

**Yields 20**

*Cantina sweets are served in open flower boats.*

Jazzy String Beans, Ritzy Beef Salad, Bootlegger's Chicken Liver Pate with Herbed Bread

All-American Peanut Butter and Jelly Cookies, Corkscrew Parfait, Flapper's Fruity Tarts

The ROARING 20's have been awakened anew and are happily kicking up their nostalgic heels all over the place as the newest of our Old Time Adventures. The Jazz Age's golden years are excitingly relived with all their bustle, pizazz, turbulence and razzmatazz. The goal was to recreate the fun, glitter and glamour reminiscent of the time when Knott's original berry stand first opened for business at the beginning of those happy-go-lucky twenties. Everybody loves it. Four sensational new thrill rides really whiten your knuckles. They are: the crowd-pleasing "Corkscrew" roller coaster with a spinning upside-down twist; the racing "Whirlwind" that circles and dips and turns at 55 per; the "Wheeler-Dealer Bumper Cars" that allow you to drive wrecklessly, legally; and "Knott's Bear-y Tales" indoor dark ride that follows the antics of a Bear-y family carrying their prize-winning jams, jellies and pies to a county fair. And it's easy to linger awhile at the Palms Casino/Buffalo Nickel Penny Arcade, rumored to be the largest game room west of the Mississippi. In this section, where the "flapper" era introduced experimentation, our recipes are more adventuresome, complex and daring.

# "Wheeler Dealer" Fruit Soup

*"Wheeler Dealer Bumper Cars" attract the youngsters.*

Surprise your guests on a hot summer night with this refreshing, vitamin-packed, chilled first course.

- ½ cup yellow raisins
- 8 orange slices, thin
- 8 lemon slices, thin
- ¼ cup lemon juice
- 1 stick cinnamon (or 1 teaspoon ground cinnamon)
- 2 cups water
- 2 cups peaches, fresh or canned, sliced
- 1½ cups cherries, pitted
- ½ cup Knott's Orange Honey
- ½ teaspoon salt
- 1½ tablespoons cornstarch

**Garnish:** 6 tablespoons whipped cream or sour cream
2 tablespoons Knott's Mint Flavored Apple Jelly

Simmer raisins, orange and lemon slices, juice, cinnamon and water in a saucepan for 15 to 20 minutes. Add peaches, cherries, honey and salt and bring to a boil. Blend cornstarch with a little of the liquid from the saucepan and add to fruit. Cook until clear, about 5 minutes. Add additional honey and cinnamon to taste.

Serve cold garnished with whipped cream or sour cream and a dab of mint jelly.

**Serves 6**

# Charleston Chicken Soup

*Everyone has a good recipe for a chicken soup — but how about a great one that includes mushroom dumplings!*

- 1  3-pound chicken or 3 pounds chicken parts (necks, backs, etc.)
  water to cover
- 2  onions, chunked
- 6  carrots, chunked
- 4  stalks celery, with tops
- 1  parsnip, chunked
- 5  sprigs parsley
  salt and pepper to taste

*A modern "Charleston" contest.*

Place all of the above ingredients in a Dutch oven and bring to a boil. Skim foam off top, cover and simmer for 1 hour or more.

MUSHROOM DUMPLINGS:
- 2  eggs, separated
- 1  teaspoon parsley, minced
- 4  tablespoons mushrooms, coarsely ground
- 2  tablespoons flour
- ½  teaspoon baking powder
- ¼  teaspoon salt
- ⅛  teaspoon pepper

Beat egg yolks until light then add parsley, mushrooms and flour mixed with baking powder, salt and pepper. Beat whites until stiff but not dry and fold into the yolk-mushroom mixture. Drop a tablespoonful of mixture into boiling soup. Cover and simmer for 10 minutes.

Serves 8-10

# Whirlwind Soup

"The Whirlwind" ride really stirs things up.

It's fun to mix ordinary vegetables in unordinary ways, as we've done with zucchini squash, leek and watercress in this soup. It's important to garnish each serving with a dollop of sour cream.

- ½ tablespoon butter
- 3 leeks, diced
- 1½ pounds zucchini, coarsely diced
- 4 cups chicken stock
- 1 bunch watercress
- ¾ cup sour cream
- salt and pepper

Heat butter in a 5-quart saucepan. Add leeks and cook until soft. Add zucchini and saute for 4 or 5 minutes. Add stock, bring to a boil and simmer uncovered until zucchini is tender, then add watercress and simmer for 5 minutes. Put in blender and blend until smooth. Season with salt and pepper to taste. Return to saucepan to reheat and add half the sour cream. Garnish with a dollop of remaining sour cream and sprinkle with chopped watercress.

**Serves 6**

# Bootlegger's Chicken Liver Pâté

*The cognac adds that special flavor to this before-dinner or salad dish. Acting as a preservative, the cognac allows you to make this tasty spread well in advance of serving.*

- 4 shallots
- ½ pound margarine, unsalted
- 4 or 5 fresh mushrooms
- 1 pound chicken livers
- ¼ cup cognac
- ½ teaspoon basil, crushed
- 1 teaspoon salt
- ¼ teaspoon thyme
- ⅛ teaspoon nutmeg
- dash of pepper

**Knott's Cucumber and Onion Pickles for garnish**

Saute shallots in ¼ pound of the margarine. Add mushrooms and chicken livers and saute for about 10 minutes or until lightly browned but still soft and pink inside. Add the rest of the margarine cut into pieces. Add cognac, basil, salt, thyme, nutmeg and pepper and cook rapidly for 1 to 2 minutes.

Pour into blender and blend until smooth. Add more seasoning to taste. Pour into crock or plastic-lined mold and seal with lid or plastic wrap and foil. Refrigerate several hours. Serve with toast and garnish with Knott's Cucumber and Onion Pickles.

**Yields 2 cups**

# Jazzy String Bean Salad

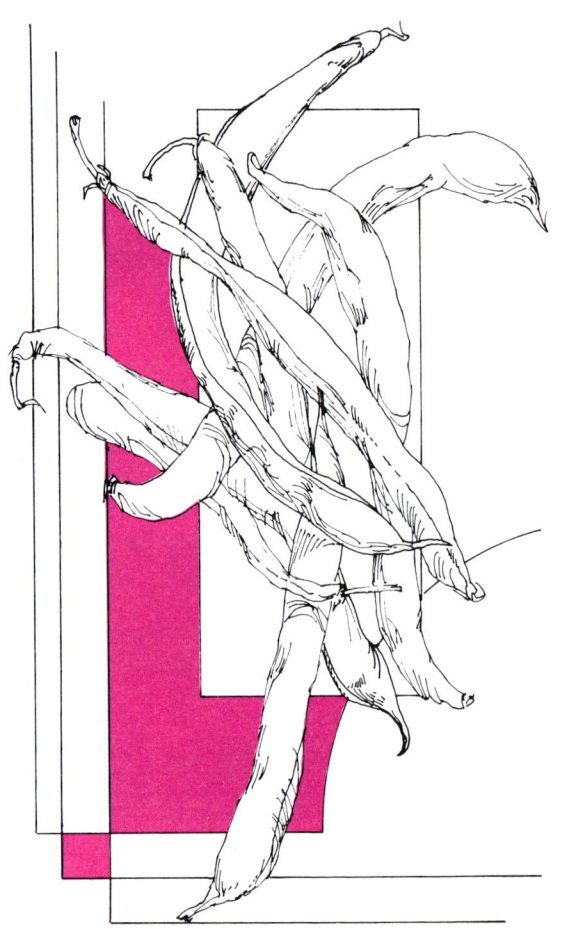

*The green string bean is ideal in this cold salad, rather than as a hot vegetable. Be sure to follow the indicated procedure to maintain the natural greenness of the beans.*

- **1 pound string beans**
- **¼ cup Knott's Italian Dressing**
- **¼ pound mushrooms, sliced pimientos**

Wash and trim ends off of beans, cutting on a slant. Cut beans in half, again cutting on a slant.

In a 3-quart pot, fill with water and bring to a boil. Drop string beans in boiling water and boil for 5 minutes or until tender but crisp. Remove with a slotted spoon to a colander and refresh under cold water. Store in refrigerator, covered, until 2 hours prior to serving. Then toss with dressing and return, covered, to refrigerator.

Serve on a bed of lettuce, garnish with sliced mushrooms and red pimientos (see "Plaza Pimientos" recipe in Fiesta Village section).

**Serves 4**

# Ritzy Beef Salad

*Here's a tasty new way to use leftover beef, and in a salad no less. Team this up with the "Herbed Bread" in this section for a smashing first course.*

- 6 cups cooked beef, thinly sliced
- 1½ cups onions, finely chopped
- ¾ cup sour pickles, chopped
- 1½ tablespoons chives, chopped
- 3 tablespoons French-style mustard
- ⅓ cup plus 2 tablespoons wine vinegar
- 2¼ cups oil
- salt and pepper to taste

Toss together lightly in a bowl the beef, onions, pickles and chives. In a small mixing bowl combine mustard, vinegar, oil and salt and pepper, mix well, then toss with beef mixture. Refrigerate until ready to serve. Serve on bed of lettuce with tomato slices.

**Serves 8-10**

# Happy Broccoli Salad

*Calorie counters have an ideal substitute for potato salad in this tasty broccoli salad. A Farm favorite, this easy-to-make salad is good for both outings and at your dinner table.*

- **2 pounds fresh broccoli, cut in 1-inch chunks**
- **1 medium onion, chopped fine**
- **1 tomato, chopped**
- **1 cup mayonnaise**
- **salt to taste**

Steam or boil broccoli until tender. Drain liquid and cool broccoli. In a large bowl, toss broccoli with onion and tomato and blend in mayonnaise. (Should you wish a more moist salad, add additional mayonnaise.) Add salt to taste. Chill well.

**Serves 6**

# Happy-Go-Lucky Rice Salad

Here's a tasty new answer to the old question of what to do with leftover rice and chicken. Great for lunches, the pineapple adds a refreshing touch.

- 1 cup mayonnaise
- 1 tablespoon lemon juice
- ½ teaspoon curry powder

- 1 cup rice, cooked
- 1½ pounds chicken breasts, cooked
- 1 cup celery, diced
- 1 13½-ounce can pineapple tidbits or 1 cup fresh pineapple, diced
- ½ cup coconuts, shredded
- salt and pepper to taste

In a small bowl blend together mayonnaise, lemon juice, curry powder and set aside.

In a large salad bowl combine rice, chicken, celery, pineapple and coconuts. Pour in the mayonnaise mixture and toss with wooden spoons. Add salt and pepper to taste and refrigerate for several hours.

Fill halves of scooped-out fresh pineapple and serve. Or serve on a bed of lettuce.

**Serves 6**

# Herbed Bread

*This bread is so flavorful that it doesn't really need a spread. Livens up any sandwich.*

  3 **eggs**
  2 **cups hot tap water (110°-115°)**
  3 **packages dry active yeast**
  9 **cups flour**
  1 **cup onions, chopped**
  2 **teaspoons dill weed (dried)**
  1 **teaspoon dill seed**
1½ **tablespoons salt**
1½ **teaspoons anise**
  6 **tablespoons parsley, minced (fresh)**
 ⅓ **cup oil**

 ¼ **cup melted butter**
   **onion salt**

In a large mixing bowl beat eggs. Add water, yeast and half of flour. Beat for about 3 to 4 minutes. Add onions, dill seed, dill weed, salt, anise, parsley, oil and remaining flour. Combine thoroughly.

Knead dough on floured board for at least 10 minutes or until dough is elastic and not sticky. Place dough in a greased bowl, grease top, cover with kitchen towel and allow to rise in a warm place until double in size, or about 1½ to 2 hours.

Punch dough down and shape into loaves, place in greased bread pans or coffee cans. Do not fill more than half full. Brush with melted butter and sprinkle with onion salt. Cover with towel and allow to rise in pans until double in bulk, or about 1 hour.

Bake in a preheated 350° oven for 30 to 35 minutes or until golden brown.

**Yields 3 large loaves**

# Boysenberry Bread

*You've had boysenberries on ice cream and in pie — now try them in bread. Fantastic!*

- 1 cup margarine or butter
- 1½ cups sugar
- 1 teaspoon vanilla
- 4 eggs
- 1 cup Knott's Boysenberry Preserves
- ½ cup sour cream
- 3 cups flour
- 1 teaspoon salt
- 1 teaspoon cream of tartar
- 1 teaspoon baking soda
- 1½ cups walnuts, chopped
- Streussel Topping (recipe follows)

Cream butter in a large mixing bowl. Add sugar and vanilla and mix until light and fluffy. Add eggs, one at a time, blending thoroughly after each addition (there's no problem if the mixture separates a little at this point). Add preserves and sour cream alternately with flour, salt, cream of tartar and soda which have been measured into a sifter. Fold in walnuts.

Pour batter into 4 loaf pans which have been greased and lightly floured. Top with streussel topping, optional. Bake in preheated 350° oven for 45 to 50 minutes or until toothpick comes out clean. Cool on rack, loosen with spatula. When cool, wrap extra loaves in foil and freeze.

**Makes 4 loaves**

STREUSSEL TOPPING:
- ¼ cup brown sugar
- 2 tablespoons flour
- 2 tablespoons butter
- ¼ teaspoon cinnamon
- ¼ cup walnuts, chopped

Combine all ingredients except nuts and mix well. Add nuts and sprinkle over batter of loaves of bread.

# Bear-y Tales Biscuits

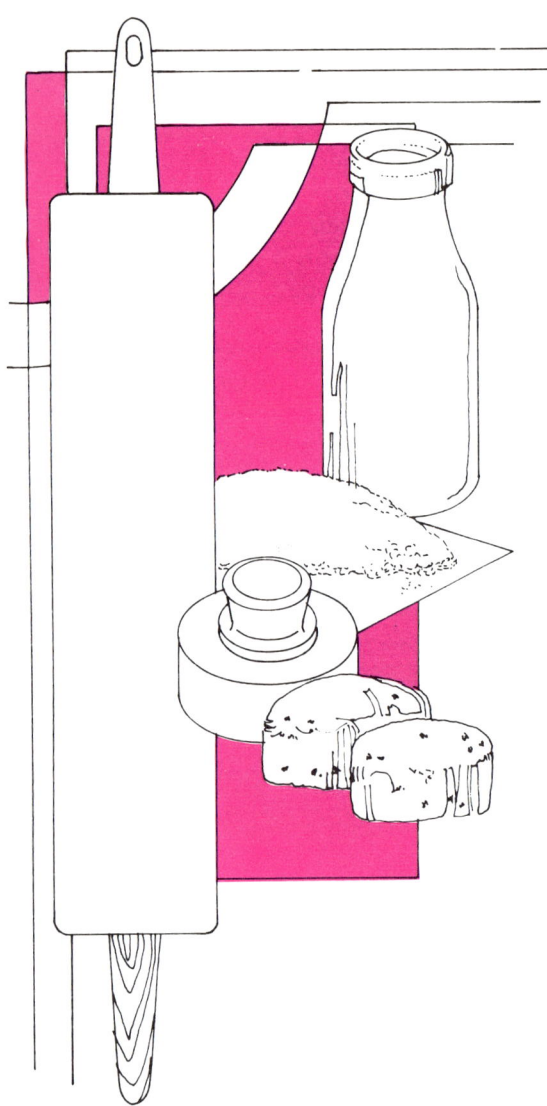

*This update of an old-time favorite is especially good at brunch or late afternoon. Serve warm, spread with any of our preserves, with your coffee or tea.*

- 2 cups flour
- 2 teaspoons cream of tartar
- 1 teaspoon baking soda
- ½ teaspoon salt
- ¼ cup butter or margarine
- ½ cup milk
- ½ cup currants

Sift flour, cream of tartar, baking soda and salt together. Cut in butter until consistency of coarse meal. Stir in milk to make a soft dough. Add currants and mix well. Divide dough in half and pat out each half on a floured board to ¾-inch thick. Cut with a 2- or 3-inch floured cookie cutter.

Bake on a greased baking sheet in a preheated 450° oven for 7 to 10 minutes or until golden brown.

Serve hot with butter and an assortment of Knott's Berry Farm marmalades or preserves.

**Yields 1 dozen**

# Speakeasy Spinach Rolls

*Wait until the next time you serve lamb to team it up with this exciting spinach side dish. The hint of mint is the perfect flavor complement.*

  1 cup olive oil
4-6 onions, chopped
  ½ cup water
  1 cup rice
     salt and pepper to taste
  ⅛ teaspoon allspice
  1 teaspoon Knott's Mint Flavored Apple Jelly
  1 tablespoon parsley
  ¼ cup dried apricots, chopped

  3 bunches large fresh spinach leaves, uncooked
14 whole dried apricots
     sweet wine
     juice of 2 lemons

Heat olive oil and add onions. Cook until soft. Add water, rice, salt, pepper, allspice, mint jelly and parsley. Mix, cover and continue cooking on low heat for 15 minutes. It should be undercooked. Cool, then add ¼ cup chopped dried apricots. Wash spinach leaves and remove stems. Pat dry with paper towels. Using one large leaf or 2 small leaves overlapping, place a spoonful of rice mixture in the center and roll stem part over filling, then fold sides over filling and roll. Continue until all the rice mixture is used.

Arrange a layer of whole dried apricots on bottom of 5 quart Dutch oven. Place a layer of torn, unused spinach leaves on top of apricots. Arrange spinach rolls side-by-side in layers. Sprinkle with wine and lemon juice, cover pot and simmer on very low heat for 45 minutes or until tender.

**Yields 3 dozen**

# Silver Slipper Stuffed Zucchini

*Add unusual new flair to some common vegetables with this uncomplicated but delicious accompaniment to your main dish.*

- 2 pounds spinach
- ¼ cup oil
- 3 anchovy fillets
- 3 tablespoons parsley, chopped
- ½ cup yellow raisins, seedless
- ¼ cup pine nuts, toasted, or slivered almonds
- salt and pepper to taste
- 2-4 zucchini or 24 mushrooms

Wash spinach and steam until wilted. Drain and chop fine.

In a saucepan, heat oil, add anchovies and parsley and cook over low heat until anchovies are dissolved. Add spinach, raisins and pine nuts and mix thoroughly with a wooden spoon. Cover and cook over low heat for 10 minutes. Season with salt and pepper.

Cook zucchini for 5 minutes, cut and scoop out seeds. Fill with the spinach mixture and bake until zucchini is soft. Or stuff large mushroom caps, sprinkle with Parmesan cheese and bake 10 minutes.

**Serves 8-10**

# Broccoli In Pastry

It's very unusual to use broccoli as a stuffing. Here we've encased it in a flaky pastry that makes this vegetable complement most main courses.

- ¼ pound butter or margarine
- 2 large onions, chopped fine
- 6 scallions, sliced
- 2 pounds fresh broccoli, washed and chopped, or 2 10-ounce boxes frozen broccoli, defrosted and drained
- ½ cup fresh dill, chopped, or 1 tablespoon dried dill weed
- ½ cup parsley, chopped
- 3 eggs, beaten
- 1 pound feta cheese, rinsed and crumbled, or ricotta cheese
- ¼ pound farmers' cheese, or pot cheese (optional)
- **salt and pepper to taste**

In a 6-quart Dutch oven, heat butter and saute onions and scallions until tender. Add chopped broccoli, dill and parsley and cook, covered, until broccoli is tender, or about 20-30 minutes. Cool.

Add remaining ingredients and mix thoroughly.

PASTRY:
- 1 cup sour cream
- ½ pound butter or margarine
- 2 cups flour
- ½ teaspoon salt

Combine all ingredients in a large bowl and blend together with a pastry cutter or fork. Form into a ball, cover with plastic wrap and refrigerate for at least one hour.

Divide into 3 equal parts and roll out on a floured board to measure 12"x6".

Spoon a third of the broccoli mixture on each pastry lengthwise, ½ inch in from the edge. Roll once and fold ends over to seal, then continue rolling up jelly-roll style. Place on a cookie sheet and bake in a 350° oven for 30 minutes. (Should you wish to freeze these rolls, butter a piece of aluminum foil and place a broccoli roll in each one and fold aluminum around roll and seal ends then freeze. To heat, open foil around roll but bottom is still on foil and place on cookie sheet and then place in a 325° oven for 30-40 minutes.)

**Each roll serves 4**

# Bloomin' Bleu Cheese Cauliflower

*Cauliflower really blooms under bleu cheese dressing. No sauces to worry about, it's all in the jar.*

- 2 tablespoons margarine
- ½ medium onion, chopped
- 1 medium cauliflower
- ¼ cup water
- 1 teaspoon basil
- 1 teaspoon salt
-   dash pepper
- ⅓ cup Knott's Bleu Cheese Dressing

Melt margarine in a large skillet, add onion and cook until tender. Cut cauliflower into 1-inch flowerettes and add to onion, mixing thoroughly to insure even coating of margarine on cauliflower. Add remaining ingredients except Bleu Cheese Dressing and cook covered until cauliflower is just tender. Stir occasionally. Add dressing and mix to evenly coat cauliflower. Do not boil — simply heat dressing and serve immediately. (Any leftovers can be served the following day chilled as a salad.)

**Serves 4-6**

# Roaring 20's Eggplant Custard

*Our tangy all-purpose dressing adds the special flavor and makes this custard extra light and moist.*

- 1 medium eggplant, peeled and chunked
- 1 teaspoon basil, crushed
- ¼ teaspoon onion powder

- 1 medium onion, chopped
- 1 tablespoon butter or margarine

- 2 eggs, beaten
- 3 tablespoons bread crumbs
- 1 teaspoon basil, crushed
- 4 tablespoons Knott's All-Purpose Dressing
- salt and pepper to taste

Place eggplant, basil and onion powder in a saucepan in 1½ inches of water and cook until tender or about 7 minutes. Remove from heat and drain well. Mash with potato masher.

Saute onion in butter until translucent and add to eggplant.

Combine remaining ingredients except for one tablespoon bread crumbs and pour into a 1-quart souffle dish or deep baking dish. Sprinkle reserved bread crumbs on top of custard. Bake in 350° oven for 1¼ hours.

**Serves 4-6**

# Satin Slipper Simple Sole

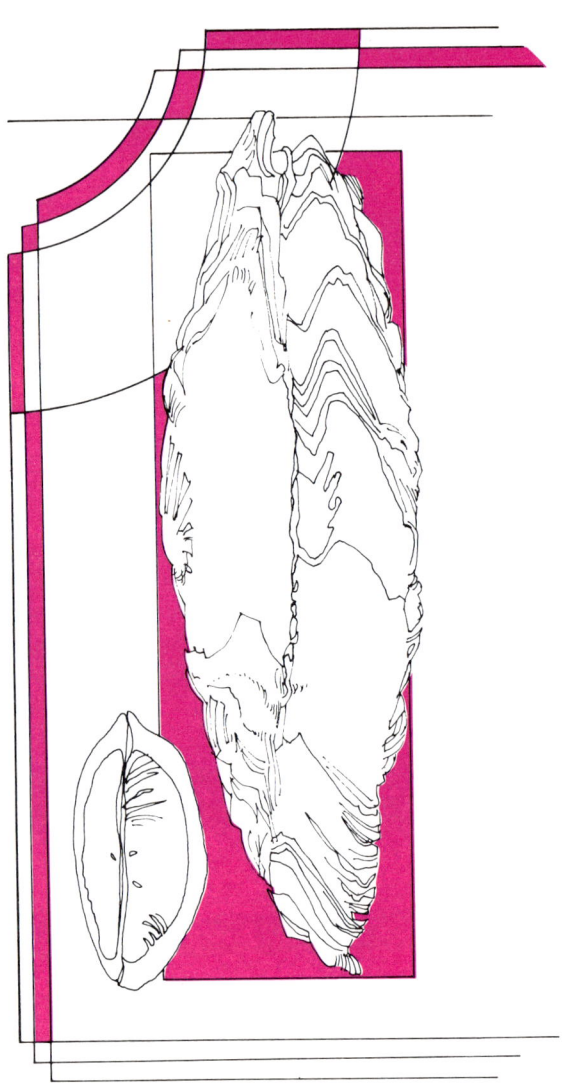

This is the simplest method of cooking fish you've ever tried! Other tomato sauces are O.K. to use, but our Knott's Steakhouse Meat Relish has a flavor difference that makes it special. Especially on this sole.

- 3 tablespoons margarine or butter
- 1½ pounds fillet of sole*
- ½ cup Knott's Steakhouse Meat Relish

Melt butter in frying pan and place fish on bottom of pan, not overlapping. Saute fillets, turning once until thoroughly cooked, about 5 minutes on each side. Spread meat relish on each fillet and cook until heated through. Goes well with "Silver Slipper Stuffed Zucchini" recipe in this section.

*Any fish fillet in the flounder family can be used in this recipe.

**Serves 6**

# Hollandaise Salmon

*Hollandaise sauce on salmon steak? Yes, because it's a natural combination.*

- **6 salmon steaks (with bone)**
- **¼ cup butter, unsalted and cut into pieces**
- **4 garlic cloves, minced**

Place salmon steaks on foil-lined broiler pan, sprinkle with pieces of butter and garlic and broil 5 to 10 minutes on each side.

HOLLANDAISE SAUCE:
- **4 egg yolks**
- **½ cup butter, unsalted, divided into 3rds**
- **2-3 teaspoons lemon juice**
- **pinch cayenne pepper**
- **¼ teaspoon salt**

In the top of a double boiler over simmering water combine egg yolks and ⅓ of the butter, mixing constantly with a wooden spoon, until butter is melted. Add the next ⅓ of butter until melted and then add remaining butter, stirring constantly. Add lemon juice, cayenne pepper and salt to taste and continue mixing over water until thick. At this point the sauce can be poured into a thermos which has been rinsed with warm water until needed.

Spoon over broiled steaks and brown for 1 minute under broiler. Serve at once with tiny new potatoes. Garnish plates with parsley and lemon slices.

**Serves 6**

# Perky Garlic Scallops

Three cloves of garlic may seem like a lot, but they're needed to perk up the usually bland scallops.

1½ pounds scallops
juice of 1 lemon

4 tablespoons butter or margarine
3 cloves garlic, chopped fine
1 medium onion, chopped
juice of 2 lemons
2 tablespoons parsley, chopped
½ teaspoon salt
1 tomato, peeled and chopped

Wash and pat dry scallops. Pour juice of 1 lemon over scallops and set aside.

In a large skillet, melt butter and saute garlic for 3 minutes; add onions and saute until soft. Add scallops, juice of 2 lemons, parsley and salt to skillet and saute turning scallops to cook on all sides. Add tomato and cook a few minutes longer. (Note: small scallops take very little time to cook and will become tough if overcooked.) Serve on a bed of steamed rice.

**Serves 5-6**

# Penny Arcade Red Snapper

Red snapper is most always available anywhere and is always good anytime. Now here's a new way to make it even better – with herbed butter and wrapped in lettuce leaves.

**Herb Butter Mixture:**
- ½ cup butter or margarine, room temperature
- 2 tablespoons fresh parsley, chopped
- 1 tablespoon fresh dill or 1 teaspoon dried dill weed
- ½ teaspoon tarragon, crushed
- 1 tablespoon breadcrumbs
- ½ onion, minced

In a blender, combine all ingredients except onion and blend thoroughly. Mix in onion (not blending).

**ASSEMBLE FISH:**
- 12 small red snapper fillets or 1½-2 pounds red snapper cut into 2″ x 4″ pieces
- 2 heads lettuce, Bibb or romaine
- ½ cup dry white wine

Spread herb butter mixture on one side of a piece of fish. Top with a second piece of fish, to make a sandwich.

Steam lettuce for 1 to 2 minutes, just to wilt. Wrap each fish sandwich with 2-4 lettuce leaves. Place wrapped fish in a greased shallow glass baking dish and sprinkle with dry white wine. Bake in 350° oven for 15-20 minutes.

Remove with a spatula and serve with steamed rice seasoned with the Herb Butter Mixture.

**Serves 6**

# Jubilant Cherry Cornish Hen

*The make-believe Keystone Kops, clowning around.*

*Most main courses aren't sweet. But here's an exceptional recipe that looks as good as it tastes. The sauce is equally tasty on chicken parts.*

- 6 **Cornish Game Hens**
  **salt and pepper**

- 3 tablespoons butter or margarine
- 1 medium onion, chopped
- 1 8-ounce jar Knott's Red Cherry Preserves
- ½ cup tomato juice
- ¼ cup soy sauce
- 3 tablespoons brown sugar
- ½ teaspoon dry mustard
- 1 tablespoon lemon juice

Place hens in baking dish and season with salt and pepper. Broil for 5 minutes on each side, watching closely so they do not burn.

Melt butter in saucepan and saute onions until soft. Add remaining ingredients and heat until preserves have melted and then bring to a boil. Pour cherry mixture over hens and bake in 350° oven for 45 minutes, basting frequently. Serve over bed of rice and spoon on cherry sauce.

**Serves 6**

# Palms Casino Orange Chicken

Here's a chicken with an exotic twist. The secret is the combination of marmalade, soy sauce and mandarin oranges. No gambling here, it's a sure bet to win compliments all around.

  2  3-to 4- pound chickens, cut in eighths
  ½  cup oil
     juice of one lemon
  1  teaspoon sweet basil, crushed
     salt and pepper to taste

  2  tablespoons oil
  1  medium onion, chopped
  1  cup Knott's Orange Marmalade
  ¼  cup soy sauce
  ¼  cup brown sugar
  1½ teaspoons sweet basil, crushed
  1  11-ounce can mandarin oranges, drained (reserve juice)

*The marquee always shines on the "Good Time Theatre."*

Place chicken in large glass baking dish or broiler pan and coat evenly with oil, lemon juice, basil and salt and pepper. Bake in a 375° oven for 12 minutes on each side. In a saucepan, combine remainder of ingredients except oranges but including juice and heat until marmalade is melted. Pour evenly over chicken and return to a 350° oven for 35 minutes, basting occasionally. Add mandarin oranges and return to oven for additional 5 minutes. Serve on bed of steamed rice.

**Serves 6**

# Razzamatazz Lamb

*A jazzy brass band in roaring form.*

*The happy blending of apples, raisins, marmalade and wine transforms ordinary lamb into an exciting adventure.*

- 3 pounds lamb, cut in 1-inch cubes
- 2 onions
- 3 tablespoons butter, unsalted
- 1½ cups white wine (or water)
- 2-3 teaspoons curry powder
- 2 bay leaves
- 2 teaspoons salt
- ¼ teaspoon pepper
- 2 apples, peeled, cored, cubed
- ½ cup white raisins, seedless
- 2 tablespoons Knott's Orange Marmalade

In a large skillet, brown lamb and onions in butter. Stir in wine, curry powder, bay leaves, salt and pepper. Cover and simmer for 30 minutes or until meat is tender. Stir occasionally. Add more wine if liquid reduces too rapidly.

Stir in apples, raisins and marmalade. Turn off heat, cool slightly and serve immediately over hot rice.

**Serves 6**

# Spicy Pork Chops

Don't just broil your pork chops. Take a little time and make them this unusual way. The apricot syrup, as the key ingredient, is the secret.

- 8 pork chops, ¾- to 1-inch thick*
- 1 tablespoon oil
- 1 teaspoon salt
- ⅛ teaspoon pepper
- ½ cup Knott's Apricot Syrup
- ½ teaspoon nutmeg
- 2 tablespoons lemon juice
- 2 tablespoons brown sugar
- ½ teaspoon cinnamon

In a large skillet, brown chops on both sides in hot oil. Pour off drippings. Season chops with salt and pepper. Mix together apricot syrup, nutmeg, lemon juice, brown sugar and cinnamon. Pour over chops, cover and simmer 45 minutes. Serve with steamed rice or cooked noodles.

*Lamb may be substituted for the pork.

**Serves 4**

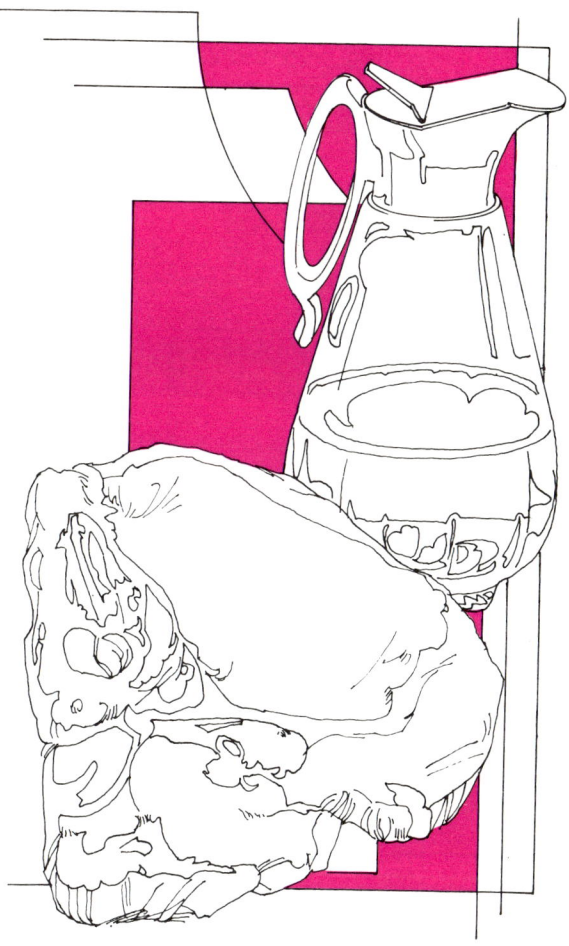

# Buffalo Nickel Ham-burger Loaf

This hamburger is really ham-burger because it combines ground ham and ground beef. The upside-down glaze is an easy trick that always works.

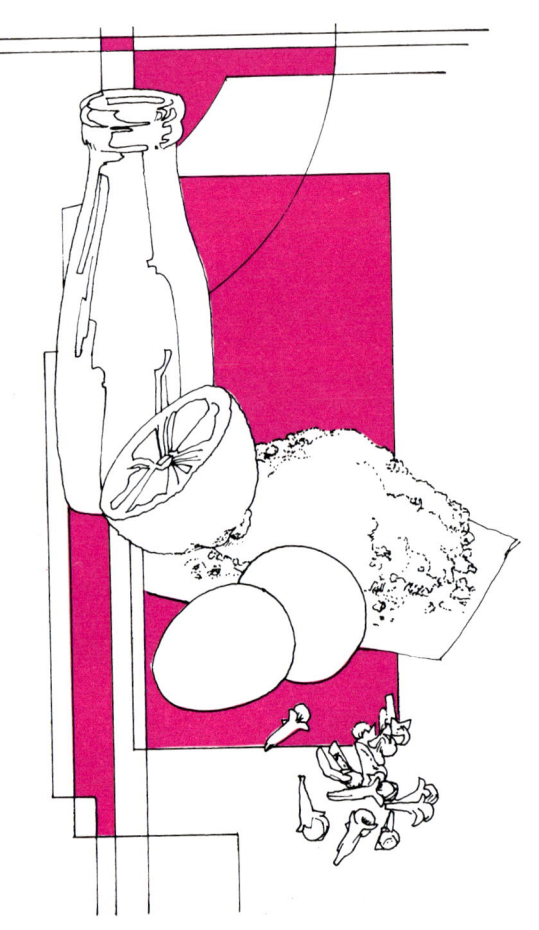

- 1½ pounds ground beef
- ¾ pound ground ham
- 1 cup bread crumbs
- 1¼ cups milk
- 2 eggs, beaten
- ½ teaspoon dry mustard

Combine all ingredients and knead together until mixture is well blended.

GLAZE:
- 1 teaspoon margarine
- ⅔ cup Knott's Apricot and Pineapple Preserves
- 8 whole cloves
- ½ teaspoon dry mustard
- 1½ tablespoons lemon juice

Grease the bottom of a loaf pan (9½" x 5¼" x 2¾" or 2 7½" x 3½" x 2") with margarine. Combine remaining ingredients in a bowl and mix well. Spread mixture on bottom of loaf pan. Place the meat mixture on the apricot and pineapple mixture.* Bake in a preheated 350° oven for 1¼ hours. Remove from oven and gently pour off any liquid. Invert on a serving plate. Garnish with parsley and pineapple slices.

*May be made in advance, covered with plastic wrap and frozen.

**Serves 6-8**

# Good Time Ham and Leek Pie

*Next time it's your turn to bring a main course dish, be different and win raves with this variation of the popular French quiche.*

- 1 9-inch flaky pie crust, baked 10 minutes and cooled

- 4 leeks, sliced thin (use only white and light green portion)
- ½ cup ham, diced
- 3 tablespoons margarine or butter

- 2 eggs
- 1 cup half-and-half
- ½ teaspoon salt
  dash of pepper

In a large saucepan, saute leeks and ham in margarine until soft. Set aside. In a bowl, beat eggs, then add half-and-half and continue beating. Add salt and pepper and mix well.

Place leek mixture into the partially baked pie crust, pour egg mixture over and bake in a preheated 350° oven for 40 minutes or until firm when tested with a knife in the center.

**Serves 6**

FLAKY PIE CRUST:
- 2 cups flour, unsifted
- ½ teaspoon salt
- 1 egg, beaten
- ⅔ cup butter
- 5 tablespoons water

Sift flour with salt into a bowl. Mix in butter, add water and egg and mix well. Knead on a floured board for 5 minutes. Refrigerate for at least 30 minutes. Roll out on floured board and place in a 9-inch pie plate or tin.

# Sticky Marmalade Sponge Cake

*This is really sticky cake, made with marmalade inside to keep it moist and sweet.*

- 7 egg yolks
- 1 cup sugar
- 1 tablespoon rind (lemon and orange)
- 2 teaspoons Knott's Orange Marmalade

- 7 egg whites
- ¼ teaspoon salt
- ½ teaspoon cream of tartar
- ½ cup sugar

- 1½ cups sifted cake flour
- ¾ cup Knott's Orange Marmalade

In a large bowl, beat egg yolks until light and add 1 cup sugar alternately with the rinds and marmalade, and mix thoroughly.

Beat egg whites with the salt until they are foamy. Add cream of tartar and continue beating until mixture forms soft peaks. Add sugar and continue beating until well mixed. Fold yolk mixture into whites until they are well blended.

Fold sifted cake flour into above mixture alternately with marmalade. Place in ungreased tube cake pan. Gently drop pan on table to remove air bubbles. Bake in a preheated 325° oven for 50 minutes. Raise temperature to 350° and continue baking for 5 to 10 minutes longer. Invert and cool. Frost with Orange Butter Icing with "13-Star Orange Bread" recipe in Independence Hall section, or sprinkle with powdered sugar.

# Corkscrew Parfait

*Imagine mixing banana and pineapple and folding them into whipped cream and you've got the basis for this luscious parfait. The chocolate sticks are easy to make and shouldn't be overlooked.*

- 1½ cups mashed bananas
- ½ cup orange juice
- ⅓ cup lime juice (or lemon)
- 1½ cups crushed pineapple, drained
- ¾ cup sugar

- ½ pint whipping cream

In a bowl mash bananas and combine with orange and lime juices. In a blender, chop pineapple into small pieces. Pour pineapple into another bowl with sugar, mixing until sugar is dissolved. Combine banana mixture with pineapple mixture and freeze for 4 hours or until mushy but not hard.

Whip cream until it forms stiff peaks. Fold whipped cream into fruit mixture and spoon into wine glasses; garnish with chocolate sticks or slices of banana and serve immediately.

**Yields 1 quart or 10-12 servings**

*The new sensation of our Roaring 20's.*

CHOCOLATE STICKS:
**1 cup semi-sweet chocolate bits**

In the top of a double boiler, melt chocolate bits over simmering water, stirring constantly. Fill a pastry bag with a star tip. Line a cookie sheet with wax paper. Squeeze out chocolate in a straight line to measure about 4 to 5 inches. Repeat until you have made 24 sticks. Refrigerate immediately. When ready to serve parfait, carefully peel sticks from wax paper and garnish parfaits.

# Flappers' Fruity Tarts

*Usually tricky to prepare, these easy-to-make fruit tarts are impressive with their professional-looking appearance.*

**Pie Crust:**
- 1 cup flour
- 1/3 cup butter and solid vegetable shortening (half of each)
- pinch of salt
- 1/4 cup chilled orange juice

Combine flour, shortening and salt and blend with a pastry blender or fork until pebbly. Add juice and work together until well blended. Do not over-work the dough. Roll out onto a floured board and cut into rounds an inch larger than cupcake size. Place each round into a cupcake pan and press firmly into place. Prick the bottom and sides of dough and bake in 350° oven for 10-12 minutes or until golden brown. Gently remove from pan when cool enough to handle and place on a wire rack. (Note: this dough freezes well if you wish to use only a portion of it.)

**Makes 12 tart shells or 1 10-inch pie shell.**

**Double recipe for a 2-crust pie.**

**Glaze:**
- 1 6-ounce jar Knott's Red Raspberry Jelly
- 1½ tablespoons lemon juice
- 2 tablespoons orange liqueur

Combine all ingredients in a saucepan and heat until jelly is melted and mixture is bubbling. Remove from heat.

**Fruit:**
- 1 8-ounce can sliced peaches
- 1 8-ounce can apricot halves
- 1 8-ounce can pie cherries

Drain each can of fruit and keep separate. Arrange the fruit in the tarts separately (do not combine them) in an attractive pattern. When glaze is warm and smooth (not hot) pour about 4 tablespoons on each tart, coating the fruit. Refrigerate tarts for at least 3 hours.

**Topping:**
- ½ pint whipping cream
- 1 tablespoon powdered sugar
- 3 drops vanilla

Whip cream until stiff. Add powdered sugar and vanilla. Place cream in a pastry bag and make a star or other design in the center of each tart.

**Yields 12-14 tarts**

# The All-American Peanut Butter and Jelly Cookie

*The natural combination of peanut butter and jelly naturally finds its way into this novel, children-pleasing cookie.*

- ½ cup butter or margarine (or ¼ cup of each)
- ½ cup Knott's Peanut Butter
- ½ cup white sugar
- ½ cup brown sugar
- 2 eggs
- ½ teaspoon vanilla
- ½ teaspoon salt
- ½ teaspoon baking soda
- 1 cup flour
- 1 cup peanuts, chopped
- Knott's Strawberry, Grape or Currant Jelly

Cream together butter and peanut butter. Add sugars; cream well. Stir in one egg, vanilla and salt. Add soda to the flour and gradually add to other ingredients. Roll dough into ¾-inch balls. Dip balls in white of one egg and roll in chopped peanuts. Place on greased cookie sheet one inch apart and press down center of each cookie with thumb.

Bake in a preheated 350° oven for 10-15 minutes or until done. Cool slightly before removing from pan to rack. When completely cool, fill center of each cookie with strawberry, grape or currant jelly.

**Yields 3-4 dozen**

Presidential Glazed Ham, Colonial Cranberry and Pear Relish, 13-Star Orange Bread

Patriot's Pumpkin Pie, Constitution Raspberry Mousse

# Independence Hall

Don't miss Independence Hall on your visit to Knott's Berry Farm. Here Walter Knott fulfilled his patriotic dream by constructing an exact replica of America's most historical building, site of the signing of our Declaration of Independence, home of the symbolic Liberty Bell, and cradle of the "greatest experiment in freedom the world has ever seen." He was thinking of the children of future generations, who could better see for themselves this beautiful reminder of our great American heritage. This imposing full-sized recreation of Independence Hall is a present-day witness to the value of freedom and independence which has descended to us by those 56 brave men who wrote: "And for the support of this Declaration, with a firm reliance on the Protection of Divine Providence, we mutually pledge to each other our Lives, our Fortunes, and our sacred Honor." Our recipes in this section reflect these exciting days of the founding of our country, with special flavors of early New England and the South prevailing.

# Liberty Bell Salmon Chowder

*Patriots gather around Liberty Bell.*

For a terrific change of tempo, try salmon in your chowder. The green pepper is the key flavor that teams up so smartly with the salmon.

¼ cup butter or margarine
⅓ cup onion, chopped
½ cup green pepper, chopped
½ cup celery, chopped
3 tablespoons flour
1 teaspoon salt
⅛ teaspoon ground pepper
4 cups milk
1 7¾-ounce can salmon, drained
2 tablespoons chopped pimientos

Melt butter in saucepan and saute onion, green pepper and celery until light brown. Add flour, salt and pepper and mix to a smooth paste. Cook over medium heat for about one minute. Remove from heat and add half the milk. Stir until blended. Return to heat, stirring constantly until mixture thickens. Add remaining milk and heat to simmering point then add salmon broken into chunks and the pimientos. Cook for approximately 5 minutes and serve.

**Serves 4-6**

# Colonial Cranberry and Pear Relish

*Have you ever heard of combining cranberries and pears? We have, and you can, in this novel, non-seasonal relish recipe.*

- 1 **package raw cranberries**
- 2 **cups sugar**
- ½ **cup water**
- 2 **pears, peeled and diced**

Place cranberries in a colander and rinse with cold water. Discard any soft or rotten berries and pour the berries into a 3-quart saucepan. Cover with sugar and water and heat over medium flame. Bring to a boil. Turn down heat and simmer until all the berries have popped. Add pears and mix thoroughly. Let stand covered until cool. Refrigerate until ready to serve.

**Yields 4 cups**

*A colonial setting.*

# Red, White & Blueberry Muffins

Our famous Independence Hall.

*These marbled muffins already have the preserves mixed right in them — just spread with butter and enjoy.*

- 5 tablespoons butter
- ½ cup sugar
- 1 egg
- 1½ cups sifted flour
- 1½ teaspoons baking powder
- ¼ teaspoon salt
- ½ cup milk
- ¼ cup Knott's Blueberry Preserves

Cream butter, add sugar and cream until smooth and fluffy. Beat in egg. Add sifted flour, baking powder and salt alternately with milk. Divide batter in half. Fold blueberry preserves into one half of batter. Spoon a small amount of batter into well-greased muffin tins, top with a spoonful of blueberry preserve batter to no more than ¾ full. Bake in a preheated 400° oven for 25 to 30 minutes.

**Yields 12**

# 13=Star Orange Bread

With a salad it would be super! And it's also great for breakfast, an afternoon tea, or even as a late evening snack.

- 1 cup orange juice, heated to lukewarm
- 1 package dry yeast
- 1 teaspoon sugar
- 1 tablespoon butter
- ⅓ cup sugar
- 1 tablespoon orange rind, grated
- 1 tablespoon Knott's Orange Marmalade
- 3 cups flour
- 1 teaspoon salt

**Orange Butter Icing**

In a measuring cup place ½ cup orange juice, dry yeast and sugar. Put remaining orange juice, butter, sugar, rind and marmalade in a mixing bowl and combine well. Pour in the yeast mixture. Add flour and salt and mix to a soft dough.

Turn out onto a floured board and knead for 5 minutes until dough is smooth and shiny. Place in a greased bowl, lightly grease top of dough, cover with kitchen towel and let rise in a warm place for 1½ hours or until doubled in bulk. Punch down. Shape into 1 large or 2 small loaves and place in greased loaf pans (1 large — 9⅝ x 5½ x 2¾, or 2 small — 8½ x 4¼ x 2½). Cover and let rise for 45 minutes.

Bake in a preheated 375° oven for 30 to 40 minutes. Remove from pan and cool on a rack.

ORANGE BUTTER ICING:
- 1½ tablespoons butter
- 1 cup powdered sugar
- 1 tablespoon lemon juice
- 1 tablespoon orange juice
- 1 teaspoon orange rind, grated
- 1 tablespoon Knott's Orange Marmalade

Cream butter and sugar together. Add juices, rind and marmalade and blend until smooth. Spread on top of bread.

**Yields 1-2 loaves**

# Southern States Spinach

*You may have to scout around a bit to find it, but the inclusion of jalapeno cheese is the key ingredient. When asking for it, remember that the "j" is pronounced "h".*

- 2 10-ounce packages spinach, chopped
- 4 tablespoons butter
- 2 tablespoons flour
- 2 tablespoons onion, chopped
- ¾ teaspoon celery salt
- ½ teaspoon salt
- 1 teaspoon Worcestershire sauce
- ½ cup evaporated milk
- ½ teaspoon black pepper
- ¾ teaspoon garlic, chopped
- 1 6-ounce roll jalapeno cheese, cut into chunks
- red pepper to taste

Cook spinach in 1½ cups water. Drain and reserve liquid. Melt butter in a large saucepan, add flour and blend until smooth. Add onion and cook until soft but not brown. Slowly add ¼ cup reserved spinach liquid, stirring constantly until smooth and thick. Add remaining ingredients and stir until cheese is melted. Combine with spinach and pour into casserole and bake in preheated 350° oven for 30 minutes.

**Serves 6-8**

# Rebel's Shrimp Remoulade

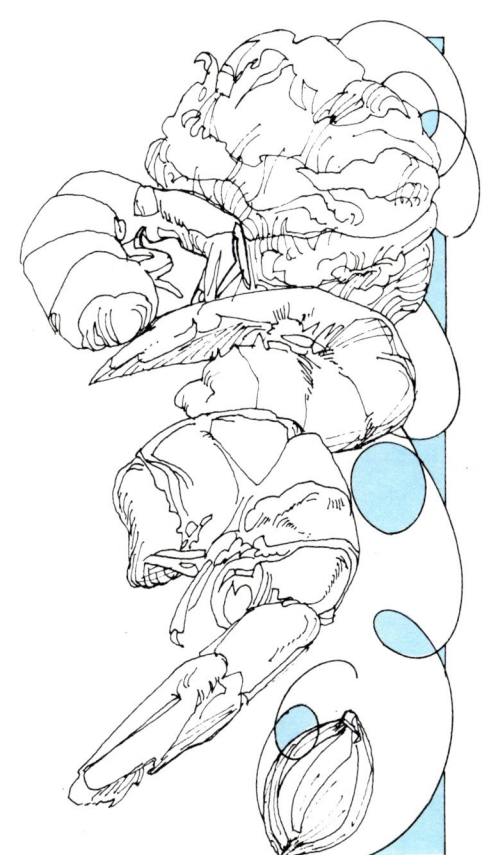

*Really liven up your shrimp with this French-inspired Southern-styled recipe. But don't substitute a prepared mustard for the horseradish mustard that "makes" this winning combination.*

- 4 tablespoons horseradish mustard
- ½ cup tarragon vinegar
- 2 tablespoons catsup
- 1 tablespoon paprika
- ½ teaspoon cayenne pepper
- 1 teaspoon salt
- 1 clove garlic
- 1 cup vegetable oil
- ½ cup green onions, chopped
- ½ cup celery, chopped
- 1 pound boiled shrimp

In a large bowl, combine first 7 ingredients and mix well. Using an electric mixer or blender, add oil and blend thoroughly. Return to large bowl and add onions and celery. Place equal amounts of shrimp on 4 to 6 lettuce-lined salad plates and spoon over a generous amount of sauce. Garnish with Knott's Cucumber and Onion Pickles.

**Serves 4-6**

# Revolutionary Chicken Pie

*Contrary to the use of the customary pie crust, this original chicken pie is topped with a cream puff pastry that is light, attractive and nourishing.*

- 3 onions, sliced
- ¾ cup butter, melted
- 2 cups rice, cooked
- 4 hard cooked eggs, sliced
- 1 2-pound chicken, cooked, boned and sliced
- salt and pepper to taste

**mock pastry**

Cook onions in 4 tablespoons butter until golden. Mix rice with 4 tablespoons butter. Butter a 10-inch pie plate and layer half the rice, onions, eggs and chicken. Repeat. Sprinkle with salt and pepper. Fill a pastry bag with mock pastry and decorate top of pie, covering top completely. Insert a metal pastry tube or small funnel in center and bake in preheated 425° oven for 20 minutes. Lower heat to 350° and bake for 20 minutes longer. Pour 4 tablespoons remaining butter through inserted pastry tube and serve hot.

MOCK PASTRY:
- 1 cup water
- ½ cup butter
- ¼ teaspoon salt
- 1 teaspoon French-style mustard
- ½ teaspoon dry mustard
- 1 cup flour
- 4 eggs

In a saucepan bring water, butter, salt and mustards to a rolling boil. Lower heat and add flour all at once. Beat with a wooden spoon until dough forms a ball and comes away from side of pan. Remove from heat. Place dough in heated mixing bowl and using an electric mixer beat in eggs, one at a time, until smooth and glossy. Or leave dough in pan and mix eggs in one at a time by hand beating.

**Serves 4-6**

# Presidential Glazed Ham

When you start with a fresh cooked ham and glaze it with this delicious sauce, you end up with an elegant main course. The secret to the success of this sauce is our apricot syrup and the Madeira wine.

- 1 4-5 pound fresh ham, cooked
- ½ cup Knott's Apricot Syrup
- ¼ cup soy sauce
- ¼ teaspoon dry mustard
- ¼ teaspoon ground ginger
- ¾ cup brown sugar
- ¼ cup Madeira

Remove as much rind as possible from ham and score side with the most fat. Place in a shallow baking dish and put in 350° oven for 5 minutes.

While ham is cooking, combine remaining ingredients in a saucepan and mix well. Heat until bubbling then reduce heat and cook until meat has completed its 5 minutes. Pour apricot glaze over ham and bake for 30 minutes, basting at least four times.

**Serves 8-10**

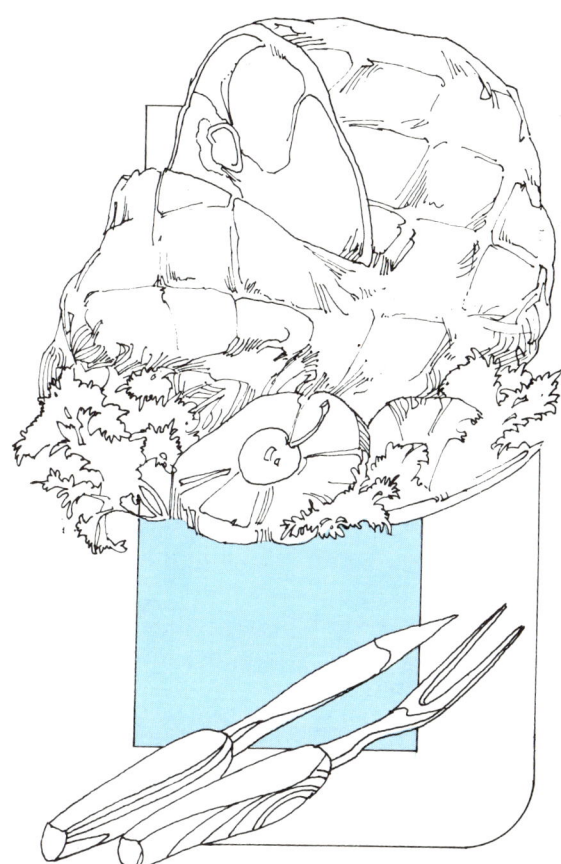

# Constitution Raspberry Mousse

*There are many steps in preparing this mousse, but do take the journey because it's well worth it.*

- 2 10-ounce packages frozen raspberries*, defrosted

- 1 envelope plus 1 teaspoon unflavored gelatin
- ¼ cup water

- 4 egg yolks

- ¾ cup sugar
- ¼ cup water

- ¼ cup kirsch, cherry or raspberry liqueur
- 2 cups heavy cream

Press defrosted raspberries through a fine sieve or strainer with the back of a wooden spoon and set aside.

In a heatproof measuring cup or small bowl pour ¼ cup of water and sprinkle in gelatin. When gelatin is softened, set cup in small skillet containing simmering water and stir over low heat until gelatin dissolves completely. Remove skillet from heat but leave cup in water to keep gelatin fluid.

Beat egg yolks with a wire whisk or electric mixer until fluffy. Set aside.

Combine sugar and remaining ¼ cup water in a small saucepan and bring to a boil, stirring until sugar is dissolved. Cook briskly, uncovered and undisturbed until a few drops in cold water form a coarse thread. Remove from heat and beating constantly, pour syrup in a steady stream into egg yolks. Continue to beat until mixture thickens and is cool. Add gelatin and mix thoroughly. Add raspberries and liqueur and mix well.

Whip cream until stiff. Mix a spoonful of cream into raspberry mixture, then fold in remaining cream until well blended but light and fluffy. Pour into well-greased individual custard cups or ramekins, or one large mold and refrigerate for 6 hours.

To serve, make a small indentation in the center of each cup and spoon in some sauce.

**Serves 6-8**

SAUCE:
- 2 cups Knott's Red Raspberry Jelly or 2½ cups Knott's Seedless Red Raspberry Preserves
- 2 tablespoons water
- 2 or 3 tablespoons sweet white wine

Melt jelly or preserves and add remaining ingredients. Spoon over mousse. (This sauce is also delicious served warm over ice cream or fruit.)

*strawberries can be substituted*

# Patriot's Pumpkin Pie

*Light and fluffy, this new pumpkin pie is so good that you needn't wait until the holiday season — it's a perfect ending to any meal at any time of the year.*

**1 9-inch pie crust, baked and cooled** (see recipe for "Flapper's Fruity Tarts" in Roaring 20's section)

- 1¼ **cups canned pumpkin**
- 3 **egg yolks**
- ½ **cup sugar**
- ¼ **teaspoon mace**
- ¼ **teaspoon salt**
- ¼ **teaspoon cinnamon**
- ¼ **teaspoon nutmeg**

- 1 **envelope unflavored gelatin**
- ¼ **cup cold water**

- 3 **egg whites**
- ½ **cup sugar**

In the top of a double boiler, combine pumpkin, yolks, sugar, mace, salt, cinnamon and nutmeg and heat, cooking for 10 minutes.

Mix gelatin and water and let stand 5 minutes. Pour into pumpkin mixture and stir until dissolved. Pour into bowl and set aside until cold. Can be put into refrigerator for a shorter time.

Beat egg whites until foamy, add sugar and continue beating until stiff enough to cling to bowl or forms stiff peaks. Fold custard (pumpkin mixture) into egg whites very carefully. Pour into cooled, baked pie crust and refrigerate. Top with whipped cream before serving.

**Serves 8-10**

# Food & Wine

## A CELEBRATION OF LIFE

BY BRIAN ST. PIERRE, *Wine Institute*

The joys of food and wine are so myriad it would take a whole book to describe them, and a lifetime to explore them — but it's a journey well worth embarking on.

Wine and food go together like ham and eggs, peanut butter and jelly, hot dogs and baseball, or John Wayne and a horse. Wine makes food taste better by refreshing the palate during the meal, is an aid to digestion and helps the body retain valuable nutrients, and makes a meal an occasion.

Unfortunately, too many Americans have allowed themselves to be pulled this way and that by snobs and self-appointed "experts" who insist that only one wine, from a particular vineyard in a special year (and made in the moonlight, for all I know), goes with a particular dish. I hope you know that this is nonsense!

The only rule is to drink the wine you like, whether it be a simple generic wine like California Burgundy or Chablis, or a varietal (made from 51% or more of a particular grape) like Zinfandel or Johannisberg Riesling. Food-wine combinations are a matter of taste and logic, and thus within everyone's capabilities. Chicken or fish cooked in an herb-and-tomato sauce, for example, would overwhelm most white wines, so a red is called for to get the best flavor balance; vinegar neutralizes wine on the palate, so it usually isn't seved with salad which has a vinegar-based dressing. It's all nicely obvious — and quite easy.

Here are a few guidelines which demonstrate the versatility of food and wine together:

**Beef** — Cabernet Sauvignon, Pinot Noir, Barbera, Ruby Cabernet, California Burgundy.

**Lamb** — Zinfandel, Gamay, Gamay Beaujolais.

**Pork** — if plain, as roasted or broiled chops, the traditional Rosé or a sturdy white like Pinot Chardonnay or Pinot Blanc; if herbed, spiced or sauced, these would do, depending on the intensity of flavor, or you could go to Zinfandel or Gamay Beaujolais. Same goes for sausages.

**Veal** — if plain, as breaded or sauteed cutlets, Pinot Chardonnay; if sauced, stewed or in any of the Italian styles, any of the reds listed with beef.

**Ham** — Grenache Rosé, Gamay Rosé, California Vin Rosé.

**Chicken** — Johannisberg Riesling, Emerald Riesling, Chenin Blanc, Grey Riesling, California Chablis.

**Turkey** — Don't worry about the little bit of dark meat; same as above, or if the stuffing is spicy, try Gewurztraminer.

**Duck and Goose** — all dark meat; Pinot Noir, Gamay Beaujolais.

**Fish and Shellfish** — Pinot Chardonnay, Fume Blanc, Sauvignon Blanc, Pinot Blanc, Dry Semillon, California Chablis.

This is but an outline which indicates the happy multitude of choices, and I hope you feel free to experiment; your palate will please you, your stomach will thank you, and your family and friends will probably worship you.

After all, as Benjamin Franklin in his infinite wisdom declared: "Wine is proof that God loves us and wants to see us happy."

# Metric System

## METRIC CONVERSION CHART

**Metric Units:**

| | | |
|---|---|---|
| 1 kilogram (kg) | = | 1000 grams |
| 1 gram (gm) | = | 1000 milligrams |
| 1 milligram (mg) | = | 1000 micrograms (mcg) |

**Weight:**

| Metric | | | U.S. Avoirdupois |
|---|---|---|---|
| 1 kilogram | = | 1000 gm | = 2.2 pounds |
| 0.1 kilogram | = | 100 gm | = 3.52 ounces |
| 0.454 kilogram | = | 454 gm | = 1.0 pound |
| 0.028 kilogram | = | 28.4 gm | = 1.0 ounce |

**Volume, Liquid:**

| | | | |
|---|---|---|---|
| 3.785 liters | | | = 1 gallon |
| 1.000 liter | = | 1000 ml | = 1.06 quarts |
| 0.946 liter | = | 946 ml | = 1 quart |
| 0.473 liter | = | 473 ml | = 1 pint |
| 0.227 liter | = | 227 ml | = 1 cup |
| 0.014 liter | = | 14.2 ml | = 1 tablespoon |
| | | 4.7 ml | = 1 teaspoon |

**Weight per Volume of Water:**

| | | |
|---|---|---|
| 1 liter = 1 kg | | |
| 1 milliter = 1 gm | = | 1 cubic centimeter |
| 1 quart = 946 gm | | |
| 1 cup = 227 gm | = | 8 ounces |

## TABLE OF MEASUREMENTS

| | |
|---|---|
| 3 teaspoons | = 1 tablespoon |
| 16 tablespoons | = 1 cup |
| 2 cups | = 1 pint |
| 2 pints | = 1 quart |
| 4 quarts | = 1 gallon |
| 8 fluid ounces | = 1 cup |
| 1 fluid ounce | = 2 tablespoons |
| 16 ounces | = 1 pound |
| 4 tablespoons | = ¼ cup |
| 8 tablespoons | = ½ cup |
| dash | = less than ⅛ teaspoon |

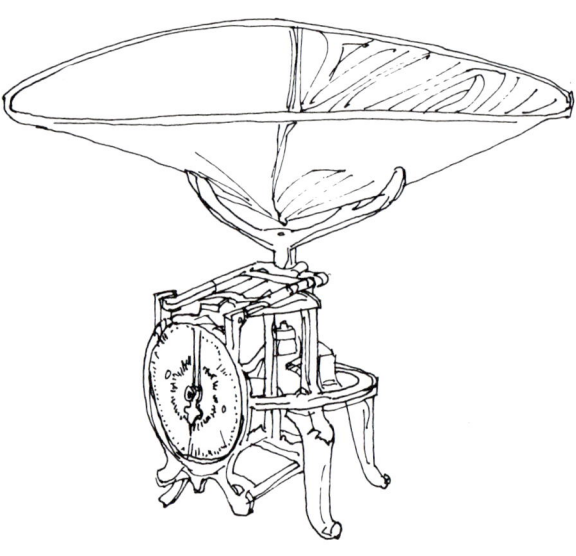

# Index

## SOUPS

| | SECTION | PAGE |
|---|---|---|
| Navy Bean Soup | Mrs. Knott's | 14 |
| Ghost Town Meal-in-a-Soup | Ghost Town | 26 |
| Main Street Cauliflower Soup | Ghost Town | 27 |
| Mexican Bouillabaisse | Fiesta Village | 56 |
| Cantina Albondigas (Meatball Soup) | Fiesta Village | 57 |
| Sopa De Ajo (Garlic Soup) | Fiesta Village | 58 |
| Wheeler Dealer Fruit Soup | Roaring 20's | 78 |
| Charleston Chicken Soup | Roaring 20's | 79 |
| Whirlwind Soup (Zucchini & Leek Soup) | Roaring 20's | 80 |
| Liberty Bell Salmon Chowder | Independence Hall | 110 |

## SALADS

| | | |
|---|---|---|
| Cherry Rhubarb Sauce | Mrs. Knott's | 15 |
| Mrs. Knott's Salad | Mrs. Knott's | 16 |
| Chicken Salad | Mrs. Knott's | 17 |
| Silver Dollar Cucumber Salad | Ghost Town | 28 |
| Campsite Corn Relish | Ghost Town | 29 |
| Russian River Eggs | Ghost Town | 30 |
| Calico Carrots | Ghost Town | 31 |
| Ceviche Ensalada | Fiesta Village | 59 |
| Jicama and Cheese Salad | Fiesta Village | 60 |
| El Pueblo Guacamole | Fiesta Village | 61 |
| Green Pepper Jelly | Fiesta Village | 62 |
| Plaza Pimientos | Fiesta Village | 63 |
| Bootlegger's Chicken Liver Pâté | Roaring 20's | 81 |
| Jazzy String Bean Salad | Roaring 20's | 82 |
| Ritzy Beef Salad | Roaring 20's | 83 |
| Happy Broccoli Salad | Roaring 20's | 84 |
| Happy-Go-Lucky Rice Salad | Roaring 20's | 85 |
| Colonial Cranberry and Pear Relish | Independence Hall | 111 |
| Rebel's Shrimp Remoulade | Independence Hall | 115 |

## BREADS

| | SECTION | PAGE |
|---|---|---|
| Buttermilk Biscuits | Mrs. Knott's | 18 |
| Farmer's Whole Wheat Bread | Ghost Town | 32 |
| Grist Mill Whole Wheat Muffins | Ghost Town | 33 |
| Masa Harina Bread | Fiesta Village | 64 |
| Happy Sombrero Sopaipillas (Fried Biscuits) | Fiesta Village | 65 |
| Herbed Bread | Roaring 20's | 86 |
| Boysenberry Bread | Roaring 20's | 87 |
| Bear-y Tale Biscuits | Roaring 20's | 88 |
| Red, White and Blueberry Muffins | Independence Hall | 112 |
| 13-Star Orange Bread | Independence Hall | 113 |

## VEGETABLES

| | SECTION | PAGE |
|---|---|---|
| Mashed Potatoes | Mrs. Knott's | 19 |
| Chicken Gravy | Mrs. Knott's | 19 |
| Cabbage with Ham | Mrs. Knott's | 16 |
| Gold Nugget Noodles | Ghost Town | 34 |
| Covered Wagon Camp Beans | Ghost Town | 35 |
| Sad Eye Joe's Squash | Ghost Town | 36 |
| Pioneer Eggplant Roll | Ghost Town | 37 |
| Gold Mine Mushrooms | Ghost Town | 38 |
| Calico Can-Can Casserole (Sweet Potato & Apple) | Ghost Town | 39 |
| Aztec Squash | Fiesta Village | 66 |
| Queso Chili Casserole | Fiesta Village | 67 |
| Castanets Cheese Casserole | Fiesta Village | 73 |
| Speakeasy Spinach Rolls | Roaring 20's | 89 |
| Silver Slipper Stuffed Zucchini | Roaring 20's | 90 |
| Broccoli in Pastry | Roaring 20's | 91 |
| Bloomin' Bleu Cheese Cauliflower | Roaring 20's | 92 |
| Roaring 20's Eggplant Custard | Roaring 20's | 93 |
| Southern States Spinach | Independence Hall | 114 |

## FISHES

| | SECTION | PAGE |
|---|---|---|
| Sage Brush Sole | Ghost Town | 40 |
| Ceviche Ensalada | Fiesta Village | 59 |
| Pescado a la Pacifica | Fiesta Village | 68 |
| Satin Slipper Simple Sole | Roaring 20's | 94 |
| Hollandaise Salmon | Roaring 20's | 95 |
| Perkey Garlic Scallops | Roaring 20's | 96 |
| Penny Arcade Red Snapper | Roaring 20's | 97 |
| Rebel's Shrimp Remoulade | Independence Hall | 115 |

## POULTRY

| | | |
|---|---|---|
| Chicken Livers | Mrs. Knott's | 20 |
| Fried Chicken | Mrs. Knott's | 21 |
| Stage Coach Stuffing | Ghost Town | 41 |
| Rancher's Marinated Chicken Livers | Ghost Town | 42 |
| Chicken a la Boysenberry | Ghost Town | 43 |
| Enchiladas con Pollo | Fiesta Village | 69 |
| Jubilant Cherry Cornish Hen | Roaring 20's | 98 |
| Palms Casino Orange Chicken | Roaring 20's | 99 |
| Revolutionary Chicken Pie | Independence Hall | 116 |

## MEATS

| | | |
|---|---|---|
| Steak House Beef Stew | Mrs. Knott's | 22 |
| Branding Iron Meatballs | Ghost Town | 44 |
| Railroad Tie Riblets | Ghost Town | 45 |
| Barber Shop Beef Fondue | Ghost Town | 46 |
| Butterfield Stage Spareribs | Ghost Town | 47 |
| Old Timer's Stuffed Veal | Ghost Town | 48 |
| Prospector's Pork Tenderloin | Ghost Town | 49 |
| Fiesta Guisado | Fiesta Village | 70 |
| Fiesta Wheels Tostadas | Fiesta Village | 71 |

| | SECTION | PAGE |
|---|---|---|
| Taquitos Verdes | Fiesta Village | 72 |
| Razzamatazz Lamb | Roaring 20's | 100 |
| Spicy Pork Chops | Roaring 20's | 101 |
| Buffalo Nickel Ham-Burger Loaf | Roaring 20's | 102 |
| Good Time Ham and Leek Pie | Roaring 20's | 103 |
| Presidential Glazed Ham | Independence Hall | 117 |

## DESSERTS

| | | |
|---|---|---|
| Mrs. Knott's Boysenberry Pie | Mrs. Knott's | 23 |
| Mother Lode Country Pastry | Ghost Town | 50 |
| Log Ride Chocolate Roll | Ghost Town | 51 |
| School House Apple Pie | Ghost Town | 52 |
| School Marm Jam Jems | Ghost Town | 53 |
| Flamenco Flan | Fiesta Village | 74 |
| Tamales Dulces (Sweet Tamales) | Fiesta Village | 75 |
| Sticky Marmalade Sponge Cake | Roaring 20's | 104 |
| Corkscrew Parfait | Roaring 20's | 105 |
| Flapper's Fruity Tarts | Roaring 20's | 106 |
| The All-American Peanut Butter and Jelly Cookies | Roaring 20's | 107 |
| Constitution Raspberry Mousse | Independence Hall | 118 |
| Patriot's Pumpkin Pie | Independence Hall | 119 |

# About the Authors

Florine Sikking and Judith Zeidler are both natives of Los Angeles, both excitingly innovative, and both natural cooks of recognized superior rank. Better yet, they both can magically translate their creative cooking ideas into a clear and simple recipe language that is enticing and entertaining. Florine is the author of several cookbooks and, teaming with Judy, has just completed another. All are published by Armstrong Publishing Company, of which Florine is a full partner along with writer-editor Carl Armstrong. Judy is a member of Chaine Des Rotisseurs, a graduate of Instituto Moderno De Lenguas Extrajeras, and teaches cooking in Los Angeles when she isn't on gastronomic trips in Europe or attending international food and wine conventions around the world.